Davis

Train up a child in the way he should go: and when he is old he will not depart from it.

BIBLE

Why is it that we, the elder, are spared to the world, except to train up and instruct the young? It is impossible that the gay little folks should guide and teach themselves, and accordingly God has committed to us who are old and experienced the knowledge which is needful for them, and He will require of us a strict account of what we have done with it.

MARTIN LUTHER

Faith in God is the source of peace in life; peace in life is the source of inward order; inward order is the source of the unerring application of our powers, and this again is the source of the growth of those powers, and of their training in wisdom; wisdom is the spring of all human blessings.

PESTALOSSI

If you follow nature, the education you give will succeed without giving you trouble and perplexity; especially if you do not insist upon acquirements precocious or over-extensive.

PLATO

It should not be claimed that there is no art or science of training up to virtue. Remember how absurd it would be to believe that even the most trifling employment has its rules and methods, and at the same time, that the highest of all departments of human effort— virtue—can be mastered without instruction and practice!

CICERO

THE SEVEN LAWS OF TEACHING

John Milton Gregory

THE SEVEN LAWS OF TEACHING

John Milton Gregory

www.VeritasPress.com
800-922-5082

The Seven Laws of Teaching by John M. Gregory, L.L.D.
Ex-Commissioner of the Civil Service of the United States, and
Ex-President of the State University of Illinois

First published in 1886

First Edition 2004

Copyright ©2004 Veritas Press
www.Veritas Press.com
ISBN 1-932168-25-7

Printed in the United States of America.

Contents

Foreword

THE AUTHOR

John Milton Gregory was obviously named by parents
familiar with and favorable toward the famous poet. Their son
greatly emulated their love of letters in his lifetime. He was
born in Sand Lake, Rensselaer County, New York, on July 6,
1822. As with most students of the time, he was educated in
locally-begun and -controlled schools, but he also excelled in
his studies and became a school teacher himself at the ripe
age of seventeen. In 1841, he began a pursuit of the law profes-
sion by attending Union College of Schenectady, New York. He
practiced law for two years and grew disenchanted with it.
Being a Christian, perhaps Gregory wanted to do more active
Christian service. In any case, he became a Baptist clergyman
somewhere in the east. Once again, however, this was not a
perfect fit. His ability to teach young people won out, and by
1852 he found himself appointed to the superintendency of a
classical school in Detroit, Michigan. (The plot thickens!)

Dr. Gregory's skills in teaching, as well as administration,
were noticed by many of his peers, and he also advocated for
their interests. He wrote for and was otherwise involved with
the State Teachers' Association, as well as being a founding
writer of the Michigan Journal of Education in 1854. This
gained him further recognition, and in 1858 he was elected to

be the state superintendent of public instruction in Michigan, a post few of his caliber would fill. So effective was his work that he was reelected twice more. He approached the work of educating children from a philosophical view, not just methodological. Yet, Dr. Gregory certainly understood the character and frame of children, as is evident in this, his most well-known work.

In 1863 he declined another term as state superintendent, wanting to get closer to the work of the classroom. Therefore, when the opportunity arose in 1864, he accepted the presidency of Kalamazoo College (in Kalamazoo, Michigan) and held that office for three years. The knowledge gained at the higher education level helped Gregory to see the critical nature of university training for students. Many universities and colleges were forming at that time across the United States. In nearby Champaign, Illinois, the Illinois State Industrial University was just being formed, and Dr. Gregory was asked to take the helm in 1867. The challenge of getting the school started well intrigued him, and he laid a solid foundation for the institution that would eventually be known as the University of Illinois. He served there for thirteen years, learning as well as guiding. While there, he also served as the United States commissioner to the World's Fair at Vienna in 1873, the commissioner from the state of Illinois to the Paris Exhibition of 1878, and a member of the board of judges in the educational department of the Centennial Exhibition in

Philadelphia. After leaving the university in 1880, he served on the United States Civil Service Commission for some time.

Dr. Gregory authored a number of books, including *Handbook of History, Map of Time* (1866), *A New Political Economy* (1882), and his masterwork, *The Seven Laws of Teaching*, first published in 1884. It was initially written for Sunday school teachers, illustrating his love of teaching and the Word of God. But he always considered his greatest service to be his work at the University of Illinois. So much so that he asked to be buried there. This request was honored after his death in 1898.

THE SEVEN LAWS OF TEACHING

Dr. Gregory, a gifted Christian man and teacher, left behind this wonderful text that would serve to benefit many teachers. However, about twenty years after its first publication, *The Seven Laws of Teaching* was "revised" by two professors from the University of Illinois in 1917, during an era of widespread liberal changes in education across the United States. Even though "every effort was made to retain both the form and substance of the original," according to the revisionists, the changes were very significant and secularizing. Virtually all references to Jesus Christ and the Word of God were expunged, along with many other alterations.

In 1983, unaware of the original work, the Logos School Board (of Moscow, Idaho) adopted *The Seven Laws of Teaching* for training and evaluating the work of their teachers. We recognized that the brilliant, concise instructions and guidance in this little book were unique in the realm of teacher training materials. For almost twenty years, we used the principles and practices contained in the book to effectively guide our teachers who, in turn, effectively taught their students, according to the truths Dr. Gregory identified and espoused so well. We also had the opportunity, with the growth of classical, Christian education across the United States, to frequently advocate the use of the book for other schools and teachers.

Then, in the summer of 2002, at a national conference of the Association of Classical, Christian Schools (ACCS), we were given a rough copy of the original, out-of-print, 1884 version of *The Seven Laws of Teaching.* Upon just a brief scrutiny, the differences were immediately apparent and amazing! In a way, those of us at Logos felt embarrassment for advocating a poor shade of what was actually a vibrant color, like encouraging the drinking of skim milk without ever knowing what whole milk was like. Needless to say, we were thrilled and humbled at the same time! We were also extremely anxious to get the original book into print again, as Dr. Gregory wrote it, so that many of our peers and even descendants could benefit from it.

How *The Seven Laws of Teaching* dove-tails with the Classical Methodology

A Consistent, Timeless View of Teaching Dr. Gregory offers us a view of a time when teaching was unabashedly absolutist in its approach. In other words, there really are right and effective ways of doing the seemingly diverse tasks associated with teaching. Like classical instruction, these laws have been with us for some time, just not in a popular or palatable manner. But they both work and work well, when studiously applied. A systematic approach to teaching is only dull and dry if the teacher makes it so. If the hands and mind are motivated by a love of truth, the students and the material, these laws become like the tools of learning, powerful tools for educating the next generation.

Applying the Natural Characteristics of Students Even before Dorothy Sayers wrote her treatise (The Lost Tools of Learning) in 1941, Dr. Gregory understood that children grow and change within identifiable levels. Teaching styles, and content to a degree, need to consider the levels to make the most of the instruction time. Dr. Gregory even taught at a classical school. He saw firsthand the advantages of knowing children well—using their experiences, senses, application, planning for the future levels.

Integration/Sequencing of Material As with classical instruction, these seven laws encourage a natural and biblical integration of knowledge and a deeper, vs. just broad, understanding of a topic. For example, the lesson must connect new to old knowledge, that's sequencing. The classical curriculum must self-consciously repeat and reinforce, sequentially, the important material and concepts. This, of necessity, will lead to doing more with less—another justification for integration.

Standards in Instruction   Too often feeling like ships at sea, teachers need a fixed beacon for evaluating the accuracy of their instruction. They need to know that their skills are not assumed, but can be guided, improved, and measured by clear objectives. This is nowhere more true than among the new breed of classical, Christian teachers. The seven laws provide a quantifiable means for both administrators and teachers to measure a teacher's skills and success.

May you find this book to be as exciting in its benefits as we have. Even in its revised version we had never seen a better book on the work of teaching than Dr. Gregory's. Having it now in its original form only makes us more convinced of its usefulness to our work as Christian, classical teachers. May God bless your teaching through your application of *The Seven Laws of Teaching.*

Tom Garfield
SUPERINTENDENT, LOGOS SCHOOL.

Introduction

Let us, like the Master, place a little child in our midst.[1] Let us carefully observe this child that we may learn from it what education is; for education, in its broadest meaning, embraces all the steps and processes by which an infant is gradually transformed into a full-grown and intelligent man.

Let us take account of the child as it is. It has a complete human body, with eyes, hands, and feet—all the organs of sense, of action and of locomotion—and yet it lies helpless in its cradle. It laughs, cries, feels, and seems to perceive, remember, and will. It has all the faculties of the human being, but is without power to use them save in a merely animal way. In what does this infant differ from a man? Simply in being a child. Its body and limbs are small, weak, and without voluntary use. Its feet cannot walk. Its hands have no skill. Its lips cannot speak. Its eyes see without perceiving; its ears hear without understanding. The universe into which it has come lies around it wholly unseen and unknown.

As we more carefully study all this, two chief facts become clear: First, this child is but a germ—it has not its destined growth. Second, it is ignorant—without acquired ideas.

On these two facts rest the two notions of education. (1) The development of powers. (2) The acquisition of knowledge. The first is an unfolding of the faculties of body and mind to

[1] Matthew 18:2

full growth and strength; the second is the furnishing of the mind with the knowledge of things—of the facts and truths known to the human intelligence.

Each of these two facts—the child's immaturity and its ignorance—might serve as a basis for a science of education. The first would include a study of the faculties and powers of the human being, their order of development and their laws of growth and action. The second would involve a study of the various branches of knowledge and arts with their relations to the faculties by which they are discovered, developed, and perfected. Each of these sciences would necessarily draw into sight and involve the other; just as a study of powers involves a knowledge of their products, and as a study of effects includes a survey of causes.

Corresponding to these two forms of educational science, we find two branches of the art of education. The one is the art of *training;* the other the art of *teaching.* Training is the systematic development and cultivation of the powers of mind and body. Teaching is the systematic inculcation of knowledge.

As the child is immature in all its powers, it is the first business of education, as an art, to cultivate those powers, by giving to each power regular exercise in its own proper sphere, till, through exercise and growth, they come to their full strength and skill. This training may be physical, mental, or moral, according to the powers trained, or the field of their application.

As the child is ignorant, it is equally the business of

education to communicate knowledge. This is properly the work of teaching. But as it is not expected that the child shall acquire at school all the knowledge he will need, nor that he will cease to learn when school instruction ceases, the first object of teaching is to communicate such knowledge as may be useful in gaining other knowledge, to stimulate in the pupil the love of learning, and to form in him the habits of independent study.

These two, the cultivation of the powers and the communication of knowledge, together make up the teacher's work. All organizing and governing are subsidiary to this twofold aim. The result to be sought is a full-grown physical, intellectual, and moral manhood, with such intelligence as is necessary to make life useful and happy, and as will fit the soul to go on learning from all the scenes of life and from all the available sources of knowledge.

These two great branches of educational art—training and teaching—though separable in thought, are not separable in practice. We can only train by teaching, and we teach best when we train best. Training implies the exercise of the powers to be trained; but the proper exercise of the intellectual powers is found in the acquisition, the elaboration, and the application of knowledge.

There is, however, a practical advantage in keeping these two processes of education distinct before the mind. The teacher with these clearly in view will watch more easily and estimate more intelligently the real progress of his pupils. He will not, on the one side, be content with a dry daily drill which keeps his pupils at work as in a treadmill, without any sound and substantial advance in knowledge; nor will he, on the other side, be satisfied with cramming the memory with useless facts or empty names, without any increase of the powers of thought and understanding. He will carefully note both sides of his pupils' education—the increase of power and the advance in knowledge—and will direct his labors and select the lessons with a wise and skillful adaptation to secure both of the ends in view.

This statement of the two sides of the science and art of education brings us to the point of view from which may be clearly seen the real aim of this little volume. That aim is stated in its title—*The Seven Laws of Teaching*. Its object is to set forth, in a certain systematic order, the principles of the art of teaching. Incidentally it brings into view the mental faculties and their order of growth. But it deals with these only as they need to be considered in a clear discussion of the work of acquiring knowledge.

As the most obvious work of the schoolroom is that of learning lessons from the various branches of knowledge, so the work of teaching—the work of assigning, explaining, and hearing these lessons—is that which chiefly occupies the time and attention of the schoolmaster or instructor. To explain the laws of teaching will, therefore, seem the most direct and practical way to instruct teachers in their art. It presents at once the clearest and most practical view of their duties, and of the methods by which they may win success in their work. Having learned the laws of teaching, the teacher will easily master the philosophy of training.

The author does not claim to have expounded the whole Science of Education, nor to have set forth even the whole Art of Teaching. This would require a systematic study of each mental faculty, and of the relation of each to every branch of knowledge, both of sciences and arts. But if he has succeeded in grouping around the Seven Factors, which are present in every act of true teaching, the leading principles and rules of the teaching art, so that they can be seen in their natural order and connections, and can be methodically learned and used, he has done what he wished to do. He leaves his offering on the altar of service to God and his fellow men.

I

THE LAWS OF TEACHING

1. Teaching has its natural laws as fixed as the laws of circling planets or of growing organisms. Teaching is a process in which definite forces are employed to produce definite effects, and these effects follow their causes as regularly and certainly as the day follows the sun. What the teacher does, he does through natural agencies working out their natural effects. Causation is as certain, if not always as clear, in the movements of mind as in the motions of matter. The mind has its laws of thought, feeling, and volition, and these laws are none the less fixed that they are spiritual rather than material.

2. To discover the laws of any process, whether mental or material, makes it possible to bring that process under the control of him who knows the law and can command the

conditions. He who has learned the laws of the electric currents may send messages through the ocean; and he who has mastered the chemistry of the sunbeam may make it paint him portraits and landscapes. So he that masters the laws of teaching may send knowledge into the depths of the soul, and may impress upon the mind the images of immortal truth. He who would gain harvests must obey nature's laws for the growing corn; and he who would teach a child successfully must follow the laws of teaching, which are also laws of the mental nature. Nowhere, in the world of mind or in the world of matter, can man produce any effects except as he employs the means on which those effects depend. He is powerless to command nature's forces except as, by design or by chance, he obeys nature's laws.

WHAT IS TEACHING?

3.   Teaching, in its simplest sense, is the communication of knowledge. This knowledge may be a fact, a truth, a doctrine of religion, a precept of morals, a story of life, or the processes of an art. It may be taught by the use of words, by signs, by objects, by actions, or examples; and the teaching may have for its object instruction or impression—the training of mind, the increase of intelligence, the implantation of principles, or the formation of character; but whatever the substance, the mode, or the aim of the teaching, the act itself, fundamentally considered, is always substantially the same: it

is a communication of knowledge. It is the painting in another's mind the mental picture in one's own—the shaping of a pupil's thought and understanding to the comprehension of some truth which the teacher knows and wishes to communicate. Further on we shall see that the word communication is used here, not in the sense of the transmission of a mental something from one person to another, but rather in the sense of helping another to reproduce the same knowledge, and thus to make it common to the two.

THE SEVEN FACTORS

4. To discover the law of any phenomenon, we must subject that phenomenon to a scientific analysis and study its separate parts. If any complete act of teaching be so analyzed, it will be found to contain seven distinct elements or factors: (1) two actors—a teacher and a learner; (2) two mental factors —a common language or medium of communication, and a lesson or truth to be communicated; and (3) three functional acts or processes—that of the teacher, that of the learner, and a final or finishing process to test and fix the result.

5. These are essential parts of every full and complete act of teaching. Whether the lesson be a single fact told in three minutes or a lecture occupying as many hours, the seven factors are all there, if the work is entire. None of them can be omitted, and no other need be added. No full account of the philosophy of teaching can be given which does not include

them all, and if there is any true science of teaching, it must lie in the laws and relations of these seven elements and facts. No true or successful art of teaching can be found or contrived which is not based upon these factors and their laws.

6. To discover their laws, let these seven factors be passed again in careful review and enumeration, as follows: (1) a teacher; (2) a learner; (3) a common language or medium of communication; (4) a lesson or truth; (5) the teacher's work; (6) the learner's work; (7) the review work, which ascertains, perfects, and fastens the work done. Is it not obvious that each of these seven must have its own distinct characteristic, which makes it what it is? Each stands distinguished from the others, and from all others, by this essential characteristic, and each enters and plays its part in the scene by virtue of its own character and function. Each is a distinct entity or fact of nature. And as every fact of nature is the product and proof of some law of nature, so each element here described has its own great law of function or action, and these taken together constitute the SEVEN LAWS OF TEACHING.

7. It may seem trivial to so insist upon all this. Some will say: "Of course there can be no teaching without a teacher and a pupil, without a language and a lesson, and without the teacher teaches and the learner learns; or, finally, without a proper review, if any assurance is to be gained that the work has been successful and the result is to be made permanent. All this is too obvious to need assertion." So also is it obvious that when seeds,

soil, heat, light, and moisture come together in proper measure, plants are produced and grow to the harvest; but the simplicity of these common facts does not prevent their hiding among them some of the profoundest and most mysterious laws of nature. So, too, a simple act of teaching hides within it some of the most potent and significant laws of mental life and action.

THE LAWS STATED

8.   These laws are not obscure and hard to reach. They are so simple and natural that they suggest themselves almost spontaneously to anyone who carefully notes the facts. They lie imbedded in the simplest description that can be given of the seven elements named, as in the following:

(1) A *teacher* must be one who *knows* the lesson or truth to be taught.

(2) A *learner* is one who *attends* with interest to the lesson given.

(3) The *language* used as a *medium* between teacher and learner must be common to both.

(4) The *lesson* to be learned must be explicable in the terms of truth already known by the learner—the *unknown* must be explained by the known.

(5) *Teaching* is *arousing* and *using* the *pupil's mind* to form in it a desired conception or thought.

(6) *Learning* is *thinking* into one's own *understanding* a new idea or truth.

(7) The *test and proof* of teaching done—the finishing and fastening process—must be a *re-viewing, re-thinking, re-knowing,* and *re-producing* of the knowledge taught.

THE LAWS STATED AS RULES

9. These definitions and statements are so simple and obvious as to need no argument or proof; but their force as fundamental laws may be more clearly seen if stated as rules for teaching. Addressed to the teacher, they may read as follows:

I. Know thoroughly and familiarly the lesson you wish to teach; or, in other words, teach from a full mind and a clear understanding.

II. Gain and keep the attention and interest of the pupils upon the lesson. Refuse to teach without attention.

III. Use words understood by both teacher and pupil in the same sense—language clear and vivid alike to both.

IV. Begin with what is already well known to the pupil in the lesson or upon the subject, and proceed to the unknown by single, easy, and natural steps, letting the known explain the unknown.

V. Use the pupil's own mind, exciting his self-activities. Keep his thoughts as much as possible ahead of your expression, making him a discoverer of truth.

VI. Require the pupil to reproduce in thought the lesson he is learning—thinking it out in its parts, proofs, connections, and applications till he can express it in his own language.

VII. Review, *review, review,* reproducing correctly the old, deepening its impression with new thought, correcting false views, and completing the true.

ESSENTIALS OF SUCCESSFUL TEACHING

10. These rules, and the laws which they cutline and presuppose, underlie and govern all successful teaching. If taken in their broadest meaning, nothing need be added to them; nothing can be safely taken away. No one who will thoroughly master and use them need fail as a teacher, provided he will also maintain the good order which is necessary to give them free and undisturbed action. Disorder, noise, and confusion may hinder and prevent the results desired, just as the constant disturbance of some chemical elements forbids the formation of the compounds which the laws of chemistry would otherwise produce. Good order is a condition precedent to good teaching.

11. Like all the great laws of nature, these laws of teaching will seem at first simple facts, so obvious as scarcely to require such formal statement, and so plain that no explanation can make clearer their meaning. But, like all fundamental truths, their simplicity is more apparent than real. Each law varies in applications and effects with varying minds and persons, though remaining constant in itself; and each stands related to other laws and facts, in long and wide successions, till it

reaches the outermost limits of the science of teaching. Indeed, in a careful study of these seven laws, to which we shall proceed in coming chapters, the discussion will reach every valuable principle in education, and every practical rule which can be of use in the teacher's work.

12. They cover all teaching of all subjects and in all grades, since they are the fundamental conditions on which ideas may be made to pass from one mind to another, or on which the unknown can become known. They are as valid and useful for the college professor as for the master of a common school; for the teaching of a Bible truth as for instruction in arithmetic. In proportion as the truth to be communicated is high and difficult to be understood, or as the pupils to be instructed are young and ignorant, ought they to be carefully followed.

13. Doubtless there are many successful teachers who never heard of these laws, and who do not consciously follow them; just as there are people who walk safely without any theoretical knowledge of gravitation, and talk intelligibly without studying grammar. Like the musician who plays by ear, and without knowledge of notes, these "natural teachers," as they are called, have learned the laws of teaching from practice, and obey them from habit. It is none the less true that their success comes from obeying law, and not in spite of laws. They catch by intuition the secret of success, and do by a sort of instinct what others do by rule and reflection. A careful study of their methods would show how closely they follow these

principles; and if there is any exception it is in the cases in which their wonderful practical mastery of some of the rules—usually the first three—allows them to give slighter heed to the others. To those who do not belong to this class of "natural teachers," the knowledge of these laws is of vital necessity.

SKILL AND ENTHUSIASM

14. Let no one fear that a study of the laws of teaching will tend to substitute a cold, mechanical sort of work for the warm-hearted, enthusiastic teaching so often admired and praised. True skill kindles and keeps alive enthusiasm by giving it success where it would otherwise be discouraged by defeat. The true worker's love for his work grows with his ability to do it well. Even enthusiasm will accomplish more when guided by intelligence and armed with skill, while the many who lack the rare gift of an enthusiastic nature must work by rule and skill or fail altogether.

15. Unreflecting superintendents and school boards often prefer enthusiastic teachers to those who are simply well educated or experienced. They count, not untruly, that enthusiasm will accomplish more with poor learning and little skill than the best trained and most erudite teacher who has no heart in his work, and who goes through his task without zeal for progress and without care for results. But why choose either the ignorant enthusiast or the educated sluggard? Enthusiasm is not confined to the unskilled and the ignorant,

nor are all calm, cool men idlers. Conscience and the strong sense of right and duty often exist where the glow of enthusiasm is unknown or has passed away. And there is an enthusiasm born of skill—a joy in doing what one can do well—that is far more effective, where art is involved, than the enthusiasm born of vivid feeling. The steady advance of veterans is far more powerful than the mad rush of raw recruits. The world's best work, in the schools as in the shops, is done by the calm, steady, persistent efforts of skilled workmen who know how to keep their tools sharp, and to make every effort reach its mark. No teacher perhaps ever excelled Pestalozzi[1] in enthusiasm, and few have ever personally done poorer work.

16. But the most serious objection to systematic teaching, based on the laws of teaching, comes from Sunday-school men, pastors and others, who assume that the principal aim of the Sunday school is to impress and convert rather than to instruct; and that skilful teaching, if desirable at all, is much less important than warm appeals to the feelings and earnest exhortations to the conscience. No one denies the value of such appeals and exhortations, nor the duty of teachers, in both day schools and Sunday schools, to make them on all fit opportunities. But what is to be the basis of the Sunday teacher's appeals, if not the truths of Scripture? What religious exhorta-

[1] Pestalozzi, Johann Heinrich (1746-1827), was a significant Swiss educational reformer, whose theories laid the foundation for much of modern elementary education.

tion will come home with such abiding power as that which enters the mind with some clear Bible truth, some unmistakable "Thus saith the Lord," in its front? What preacher wins more souls than Moody with his open Bible ever in hand? What better rule for teacher or pupil than the Master's "Search the Scriptures?"[2] What finer example than that of Paul who "reasoned" with both prejudiced Jews and caviling Greeks "out of the Scriptures?"[3] If the choice must be between the warm-hearted teacher who simply gushes appeals, and the cold-hearted who stifles all feeling by his icy indifference, give me the former by all odds; but why either? Is there no healthful mean between steam and ice for the water of life? Will the teacher whose own mind glows with the splendid light of divine truths, and who skillfully leads his pupils to a clear vision of the same truths, fail in inspirational power? Is not the divine truth itself—the very Word of God—to be credited with any power to arouse the conscience and convert the soul?

17. These questions may be left to call forth their own inevitable answers. They will have met their full purpose if they repel this disposition to discredit the need of true teaching-work, in Sunday-schools as well as in common schools; and if they convince Sunday school leaders that the great natural laws of teaching are God's own laws of mind, which must be followed as faithfully in learning His Word as in studying His works.

[2] John 5:39   [3] Acts 17:2

A WORD TO TEACHERS

18. Leaving to other chapters the full discussion of the meaning and philosophy of these seven laws, we only add here the exhortation to the teacher, and especially to the Sunday school teacher, to give them the most serious attention. Sitting before your class of veiled immortals, how often have you craved the power to look into the depths of those young souls, and to plant there with sure hand some truth of science or some grand and life-giving belief of the gospel? How often have you tried your utmost, by all the methods you could devise, to direct their minds to the deep truths and facts of the Bible lesson, and turned away, almost in despair, to find how powerless you were to command the mental movement and to secure the spiritual result? No key will ever open to you the doors of those chambers in which live your pupils' souls; no glass will ever enable you to penetrate their mysterious gloom. But in the great laws of your common nature lie the electric lines by which you may send into each little mind the thought fresh from your own, and awaken the young heart to receive and embrace it. He who made us all of kindred nature settled the spiritual laws by which our minds must communicate, and made possible that art of arts which passes thought and truth from soul to soul.

19. *Remark.* In the discussion of these laws there will necessarily occur some seeming repetitions. They are like

seven hilltops of different height scattered over a common territory. As we climb each in succession, many points in the landscapes seen from their summits will be found included in different views, but it will be always in a new light and with a fresh horizon. The truth that is common to two or more of these laws will be found a mere repetition. New groupings will show new relations and bring to light for the careful student new aspects and uses. The repetitions themselves will not be useless, as they will serve to emphasize the most important features of the art of teaching, and will impress upon the younger teachers those principles which demand the most frequent attention.

II

THE LAW OF THE TEACHER

1. The universal reign of law is the central truth of modern science. No force in man or nature but works under the control of law; no effect in mind or matter but is produced in conformity with law. The simplest notion of natural law is that nature remains forever uniform in its forces and operations. Causes compel their effects, and effects obey their causes, by irresistible laws. Things are what they are by reason of the laws of their being, and to learn the law of any fact is to learn the deepest truth we can know about it. This uniformity of nature is the basis of all science and of all practical art. In mind and in matter the reign of unvarying laws is the primal condition of any true science. The mind, indeed, has its freedoms, but among these there is found no liberty to produce effects contrary to laws. The teacher is therefore as

much the subject of law as the star that shines or the ship that sails. Many qualifications are easily recognized as important to the teacher's position and work; and if all the requirements popularly sought for could be obtained, the teacher would be a model man or woman; perfect in manners, pure in morals, unerring in wisdom, just in judgment, loving in temper, firm in will, tireless in work, conscientious in word and deed, a genius in learning, an angel in charity, an incarnate assemblage of impossible excellencies. Certainly, good character and rare moral qualities are desirable in an instructor of the young, if not for his actual work, at least to prevent harm from his example; but if, one by one, we dismiss from our catalogue of needful qualifications for the work of teaching those not absolutely indispensable, we shall find ourselves obliged to retain at last, as necessary to the very notion of teaching, a knowledge of the branches to be taught. The Law of the Teacher, then—the law which limits and describes him—is this:

The teacher must know that which he would teach.

PHILOSOPHY OF THE LAW

2.   It seems too simple for proof that one can not teach without knowledge. How can something come out of nothing, or how can darkness give light? To affirm this law seems like declaring a truism; but deeper study shows it to be a fundamental truth—the very law of the teacher's action and being as a teacher. No other characteristic or qualification is

so fundamental and essential. The law will reveal a deeper truth if we reverse its terms and read: What the *teacher knows he must teach.* There is an inborn need and desire in man for expression. It is the instinctive impulse to tell in some way, by word or action, our thoughts and emotions so soon as they become vivid and intense enough. It is the teaching passion. "While I was musing the fires burned: then spake I with my tongue."[1] Other motives and impulses may mingle and aid, but this is primary and fundamental. The hot heart—hot with visions and discovered truth—forces speech, or teaching which is better than speech.

3.   The word *know* stands central in the law of the teacher. *Knowledge* is the material with which the teacher works, and the first reason of the law must be sought in the nature of knowledge. What men call knowledge is of all degrees, from the first dim glimpse of a fact or truth to the full and familiar understanding of that fact or truth in all its parts and aspects —its philosophy, its beauty, and its power. (1) We may know a fact so faintly as merely to recognize it when another tells it; (2) we may know it in such degree as to be able to recall it for ourselves, or to describe it in a general way to another; (3) better still, we may so know it that we can readily explain, prove, and illustrate it; or (4), mounting to the highest grade of knowledge, we may so know and vividly see a truth in its deeper significance and wider relations that its importance,

[1] Psalm 39:3

grandeur, or beauty impresses and inspires us. History is history only to him who thus reads and knows it; and Scripture is Holy Writ only when seen by this inner light. It is this last form of knowledge which must be read into the law of the true teacher.

4.   It is not affirmed that no one can teach without this fullness of knowledge; nor is it true that every one who knows his lessons thus thoroughly will teach successfully. But imperfect knowing must make imperfect teaching. What a man does not know he can not teach, or, if he teaches, can not know that he teaches. But the law of the teacher is only one of the laws of teaching. Failure may come from the violation of other conditions as well as from neglect of this. So, too, success may come from obedience to other laws. A poor, illiterate mother may so inspire the ambition of her boy that he will work out his lessons from a book without a teacher. Many a teacher can do little more than to study up the lesson of the day, and may use that skillfully to set his pupils to work; but teaching must be uncertain and limping with such limitations of knowledge.

5.   A truth can be fully seen only in the light of other truths. It is known by its resemblances. A fact which is only partly known never reveals its thousand beautiful analogies to other facts. It stands alone, beclouded and barren—half fact and half phantom. The eye catches no fine resemblances, and the understanding finds no fruitful relations, linking it to the

great body of truth. The imagination looks in vain for the light of some rich and beautiful simile to transfigure the truth seen only in dim outline, or known only in shapeless and imperfect fragments. Only amid facts vividly seen, and among truths clearly and splendidly conceived, are to be discovered the images of grander facts and the shadowy forms of wider truths. The power of illustration—that chief and central power in the teacher's art—comes only out of clear and familiar knowledge. The unknowing teacher is the blind trying to lead the blind with only an empty lamp to light the way.[2]

6.   Take the common facts taught in the geographies of the schools,—the roundness of the earth, the extent of oceans and continents, mountains, rivers, and peopled states and cities,— how tame and slight in interest as known to the half-taught teacher and his pupils; but how grand and imposing as seen by the great astronomers, geologists, and geographers— the Herschels,[3] Danas,[4] and Guyots![5] To these appear in vision the long processions of age-filling causes and revolutions which have not only given shape to this enormous globe, but have peopled the boundless universe with countless millions of similar and still grander spheres—causes which yet move and work in the ceaseless march of suns and systems, in the

[2] Matthew 15:14
[3] Herschel, William (1738-1822), discovered Uranus.
[4] Dana, James Dwight (1813-1895), American mineralogist, born in Utica, New York, and educated at what is now Yale University. He explored much of the Antarctic in 1838.
[5] Guyot, Arnold (1807-1884), founded Princeton Museum of Natural History.

perpetual roll of the earth's revolutions, in the swing of tides, the sweep of winds and storms, the flow of rivers, the slow heave of the continents, the incessant climatic changes and seasons, and in all the various births, growths, and decays of nature and mankind. To such teachers geography is but a chapter in the science and history of the universe, borrowing light and meaning from all that goes before or follows. So, too, the great texts and truths of Holy Writ: how meager in meaning to the careless reader and the unstudious teacher! but how brilliant and burning with divine fact and truths to him who brings to its study the converging lights of history, science, and experience!

7.   But the law of the teacher goes deeper still. Truth must be clearly understood before it can be vividly felt. Only the true scholars in any science grow enthusiastic over its glories and grandeurs. It is the clearness of their mental vision which inspires the wonderful eloquence of the poet and orator, and makes them the born teachers of their race. It was Hugh Miller, the deep-read geologist, whose trained eye deciphered, and whose eloquent pen recorded "The Testimony of the Rocks."[6] Kepler, the great astronomer, grew wild as the mysteries of the stars unrolled before him, and Agassiz[7] could not afford time to lecture for money while absorbed in the

[6] Miller, Hugh (1802-1856), Scottish geologist and popular author.
[7] Agassiz, (Jean) Louis Rodolphe (1807-1873), Swiss-American naturalist, born in Motiers, Switzerland. He was able to bring a great amount of public interest to natural science in his day.

deep study of the old dead fishes of an ancient world. He must ever be a cold and lifeless teacher who only half knows the lessons he would teach; but he whose soul has caught fire from the truths which he carries, glows with a contagious enthusiasm and unconsciously inspires his pupils with his own deep interest. "Much learning doth make thee mad,"[8] said the half-startled Festus, as Paul, the great apostle, told with irrepressible warmth the story so vivid in his remembrance, so fresh in his feeling.

8. This earnest feeling of truths clearly and grandly conceived is the very secret of the earnestness and enthusiasm so much praised and admired in teacher and preacher. Even common truths become transformed and grand in the mind and heart of such a teacher. History turns to a living panorama; geography swells out into great continental stretches of peopled kingdoms; astronomy becomes the marshaled march of shining worlds and world-systems, and Bible truths grow sublime as with the felt presence of Deity. How can the teacher's manner fail to be earnest and inspiring when his matter is so rich with radiant reality?

9. While knowledge thus thoroughly and familiarly known rouses into higher action all the powers of the teacher, it also gives him the unfettered command and use of those powers. Instead of the hurry and worry of one who has to glean from the textbook each moment the answers to the

[8] Acts 26:24

questions he has asked, he who knows his lesson as he ought is at home, on familiar ground, and can watch at ease the efforts of his class and direct with certainty the current of their thoughts. He is ready to recognize and interpret their first faint glimpses of the truth, to remove the obstacles from their path, and to aid and encourage their struggling search by the skillful hint which flashes a half-revealing light into the too thick darkness.

10. A teacher's ready and evident knowledge helps to give the pupil needed confidence. We follow with eager expectation and delight the guide who shows thorough knowledge of the field we wish to explore, but we drag reluctantly and without interest after an ignorant and incompetent leader. Children instinctively object to being taught by one whom they have found to be ignorant or unready in their lessons, just as soldiers refuse to follow an incompetent commander. Nor is this all. As the great scholars, the Newtons,[9] the Humboldts,[10] and the Huxleys,[11] kindle public interest in the sciences which lend them their renown, so the ripe knowledge of the well-prepared teacher awakens in his class the active desire to know more of the studies in which he is proficient. Science and religion are never so attractive as when seen

[9] Newton, Sir Isaac (1642-1727), the well-known English physicist, mathematician and natural philosopher. He is still considered one of the most important scientists of all time, basing his ideas on a biblical view of the world.
[10] Humboldt, Alexander von (1769-1859), famed natural scientist.
[11] Huxley, Thomas Henry (1825-1895), nicknamed "Darwin's Bulldog." One of the first adherents to and popular champion of Darwin's theory of evolution.

through a living scholar or Christian. And yet it must be confessed that the ability to inspire pupils with a love of study is sometimes lacking even where great knowledge is possessed; and this lack is fatal to all successful teaching, especially among young pupils. Better a teacher with limited knowledge but with this power to stimulate his pupils than a very Agassiz without it. The cooped hen may by her encouraging cluck send forth her chickens to the fields she cannot herself explore; but sad the fate of the brood if they remain in the coop while she goes abroad to feed.

11. Such is the profound philosophy, the wide and generous meaning, of this first great law of teaching. Thus understood, it clearly portrays the splendid ideal which no one except the Great Teacher ever fully realized, but which every true teacher must more or less nearly approach. It defines with scientific certainty the forces with which the successful teacher must go to his work. From the mother teaching her child to talk, to the highest teacher of science, the orator instructing listening senates, and the preacher teaching great congregations, this law knows no exceptions and allows no successful violations. It affirms everywhere, *the teacher must know that which he would teach.* Out of this one fundamental law must arise every practical rule to guide the teacher in preparing for his work.

Rules for Teachers

12. Among the rules which arise out of the Law of the Teacher, the following are the most important:

(1) Prepare each lesson by fresh study. Last year's knowledge has necessarily faded somewhat. Only fresh conceptions warm and inspire us.

(2) Seek in the lesson its analogies and likenesses to more familiar truths. In these lie the illustrations by which it may be taught to others.

(3) Study the lesson till its thoughts take shape in familiar language. The final proof and product of clear thought is clear speech.

(4) Find the natural order and connection of the several facts and truths in the lesson. In every science there is a natural path of ascent, from its simplest notions to its sublimest outlooks. So, too, in every lesson. The temple of truth is not a jumbled mass of disjointed facts.

(5) Seek the relation of the lesson to the lives and duties of the learners. The practical value of truth lies in these relations.

(6) Use freely all aids, but never rest till the truth rises clear before you as a vision seen by your own eyes.

(7) Ask for *all* the facts and views of a subject, but be sure to master *some*. Better to know one truth well than to know a hundred imperfectly.

(8) Have a time for the study of each lesson, and, if possible, some days in advance of the teaching. All things help the duty done on time, but all things hinder or hurry the duty out of time. The mind keeps on studying the lesson learned in advance, and gathers fresh interest and illustrations.

(9) Have a plan of study, but study beyond the plan. I once suggested as an artificial but helpful plan for the study of a Bible lesson the letters of the word BIBLE. B—Book in which the lesson is found, with its date, author, object, and contents or scope. I—Intention of the lesson; the included facts, and the interpretation of those facts. B—Blessings and Benefits to be gained from the lesson. L—Losses likely to follow from a failure to learn and obey. E—Examples, Experiences, and Exhortation. Let the teacher address each point as a question to his own mind, and think till he gets an answer —and an answer that is true. The three questions What? How? and Why? afford a more perfect mnemonic, calling for more scientific research and applying to all branches of knowledge.

(10) Do not deny yourself the help of good books on the subject of the lessons. Buy, borrow, or beg, if necessary, but get the help of the best scholars and thinkers, enough at least to set your own thoughts going; but do not read without deep and original thinking.

If possible, talk your lesson over with an intelligent friend. Collision often brings light. In the absence of these aids, write your views. The nib of the pen digs deep into the mines of truth. Expressing thought often clears it of its dross and obscurities.

VIOLATIONS AND MISTAKES

13. The discussion would be incomplete without some notice of the frequent violations of the law. Someone has said: "The secret of success is to make no mistakes." Certain it is that the best teacher may spoil his most careful and earnest work by some small and careless blunder.

(1) The very ignorance of his pupils often tempts the teacher to neglect all preparation and study. He thinks that at any rate he will know much more of the lesson than the children can, and counts that he will find something to say about it, or that at worst his ignorance will pass unnoticed. A sad mistake, and often costing dear! Some bright or studious pupil is almost sure to discover the cheat, and henceforth that teacher's credit with his class is gone.

(2) Some teachers assume that it is the pupils' work, not theirs, to study the lesson; and that with the aid of the book in hand, they will easily enough be able to ascertain if the children have done their duty. Better let one of the pupils who knows his lesson examine the

others, and sit by as a learner, rather than discourage study by your too evident ignorance and indifference.

(3) Others look hastily through the lesson, and conclude that though they have not mastered it, nor perhaps one thought in it, they have gathered enough to fill the brief hour, and they can, if needful, eke out the little they know with random talk or story. Or, lacking time or heart for any preparation, they carelessly dismiss all thought of teaching, fill the hour with such exercises as may occur to them, and hope that, as the Sunday school is a good thing, the children will get some good from mere attendance.

(4) A more serious fault is that of those who, failing to find anything in the lesson, try to graft something upon it, and make it a mere cart to carry their own fancies on.

(5) There is a meaner, if not also a more mischievous, wrong done by the teacher who seeks to conceal his lazy ignorance by some pompous pretence of learning, hiding his lack of knowledge by an array of high-sounding words beyond the comprehension of his pupils, uttering solemn platitudes in a wise tone, or claiming extensive study and profound information which he has not the time to lay properly before them. Who has not seen or heard all these shams practiced upon children?

Thus a majority, perhaps, of teachers go to their work either wholly without the requisite knowledge, or only partly prepared for their task. They go like messengers without a message, and all wanting in that power and enthusiasm which fresh truth alone can give; and so the grand fruits we look for from this great army of workers seem long in coming, if not beyond hope. Let this first great fundamental law of teaching be thoroughly obeyed, or even as fully as the circumstances of our teachers will permit, and there will come to our schools an attractive charm which would at once increase their numbers and double their usefulness. The schoolrooms, now so often dark and dull, would glow as with a living light, and teachers and pupils, instead of dragging to their weary task, would hasten to their meeting as to a joyous feast.

III

THE LAW OF THE LEARNER

1. Passing from the side of the teacher to the side of the pupil,
our next inquiry is for the Law of the Learner. Here the search
must be for that one characteristic, if there be such, which
divides and differentiates the learner from other persons—for
that essential element which makes the learner a learner. Let
us place before us the successful scholar, and note carefully
whatever is peculiar and essential in his action and attributes.
His intent look, his absorbed manner, his face full of eager
action or of profound study—all these are but so many signs
of deep interest and active attention. This interest and
attention, the inseparable parts of one mental state, make up
the essential attribute of every true learner. The very power to
learn lies in this interested attention. It is the one essential
condition on which all learning is possible. It constitutes,

therefore, the natural law of the learner, and may be stated in preceptive form as follows:

The learner must attend with interest to the fact or truth to be learned.

2.   The law thus stated will seem as trite as a common truism, but it is as really profound as it is seemingly simple. The plainest proof of its truth lies in the readiness with which everyone will admit it. Its real depth can only be found by careful study.

ATTENTION DESCRIBED

3.   Avoiding as much as possible all metaphysical discussion, we may describe attention as a mental attitude—the attitude in which the thought-power is actively bent toward, or fastened upon, some object of thought or perception. It is an attitude, not of ease and repose, but of effort and exertion. It means not merely position and direction, but action. It is the will-power marshaling all the faculties of the mind for some expected onset, or holding them with steady front in the midst of conflict and activity. It may be seen in the man who, standing with idle, vacant stare, gazing at nothing, is suddenly aroused by some sight or sound. At once a light comes into the eye, the look becomes alert, and the mind is put into conscious action. There is a felt strain of the thinking faculty, as of an appetite hungering for its food—an intent fastening of the intellect upon its chosen objects. This aroused activity of the

mind—this awakened attitude of mental power, poised and eager for its work—we call ATTENTION.

COMPELLED AND ATTRACTED ATTENTION

4.   We may somewhat loosely divide attention into two classes: *compelled* and *attracted.* The first is given by an effort of the will, in obedience to some command of authority, or call of irksome duty; the second springs from desire, and is given without conscious effort and with eager delight. The first is cold, mechanical, and powerless; it is the child studying its lesson as a task, with slight interest and no pleasure. The second is living and full of power, the mind eager to grasp and possess its object. It is that of the boy reading a story full of wonder and delight. Compelled attention in adults is dull and dogged; in little children it is partial even when possible. Generally it is not attention at all. The face may take on the look of attention, but the mind wanders to more winsome objects. It learns to hate lessons as slaves hate labor. Attracted attention is mental power alert with desire and eager for gratification. It is mental hunger seeking its food, and delighting itself as at a feast. Unconscious of exertion, it gathers strength from its efforts, and scarcely knows fatigue.

5.   Compelled attention is short-lived and easily exhausted. Its very painfulness wearies the powers of body and mind. If urged too far, its tension breaks, and the child yawns and even sleeps with exhaustion, or cries with pain and

anger. Attracted attention, on the other hand, is full of power and endurance. Its felt interest calls dormant energies into play, and the pleasure given by its efforts seems to refresh rather than weary the mind. The boy forced to study what he does not like feels thoroughly tired in half an hour. Give him now a story which he enjoys, and he will read without a sign of weariness for two or three hours longer, till the tired body rebels, and will not sit still any longer.

6.   At times in the outset of a lesson or of a subject, there may seem a need of securing the attention of the class or of some members of it by a gentle compulsion, an appeal to the sense of duty, or other like means; but the effort in such case should be made to transform this compelled attention into that which is fuller of spontaneity and power. We may be obliged to lift a sleepy child to his feet by main strength, but unless we can waken him soon to walk by himself, his progress will be slow and small. The same holds true in mental movements.

DEGREES OF ATTENTION

7.   These two classes of attention melt into each other by almost insensible degrees. The compelled sometimes rises into true or attracted attention by some kindling of interest in the subject; and not infrequently the latter sinks into the former with the disappearance of novelty in the lesson. Of these degrees or grades in attention, the first and lowest is that

in which the physical senses, the eye and ear especially, are lent to the teacher, and the mind almost passively receives what the teacher is able to impress forcibly upon it. This grade of attention is too common to need description. It may be seen in nearly all schoolrooms, and in most classes at the beginning of the lesson. The pupils sit at ease waiting to be aroused.

8.   From this lowest grade the intellect lifts itself by successive steps to higher activity and power under some impulse of duty, of sympathy, of emulation, or of hope of reward, or other motives addressed to it by the skillful teacher. But the highest grade of attention is that in which the subject interests, the feeling is enlisted, and the whole nature attends. Eye, ear, intellect, and heart concenter their powers in a combined effort, and the soul sends to the task all its faculties roused to their utmost activity. Such is the attitude of the true learner, and such is the attention demanded by this law of the learner in its perfect fulfillment. Every experienced teacher knows how easy is the teaching, and how rapid the learning, when the law is thus fulfilled.

THE PHILOSOPHY OF THE LAW

9.   However much teachers may neglect it in practice, they readily admit in theory that without attention the pupil can learn nothing. One may as well talk to the deaf or the dead as to teach a child who is wholly inattentive. All this seems too obvious to need discussion; but a brief survey of the psycholog-

ical facts which underlie this law will bring out into clearer and more impressive light its vital force and its irrevocable authority.

10. Knowledge cannot be passed, like some material substance, from one person to another. Thoughts are not things which may be held and handled. They are the unseen and silent acts of the invisible mind. Ideas, the products of thought, can only be communicated by inducing in the receiving mind action correspondent to that by which these ideas were first conceived. In other words, ideas can only be transmitted by being rethought. It is obvious, therefore, that something more is required than a passive presentation of the pupil's mind to the teacher's mind as face turns to face. The pupil must think. His mind must work, not in a vague way, without object or direction, but under the control of the will, and with a fixed aim and purpose; in other words, with attention. It is not enough to look and listen. The learner's mind must work through the senses. There must be mind in the eye, in the ear, in the hand. If the mental power is only half aroused and feeble in its action, the conceptions gained will be faint and fragmentary, and the knowledge acquired will be as inaccurate and useless as it will be fleeting. Teacher and textbook may be full of knowledge, but the learner will get from them only so much as his power of attention, vigorously exercised, enables him to shape in his own mind. Knowledge is inseparable from the act of knowing. If the power of knowing is small, the actual knowledge acquired will also be small.

11. The notion that the mind can be made merely recipient —a bag to be filled with other people's ideas, a piece of paper on which another may write, a cake of wax under the seal—is neither safe nor philosophical. The very nature of mind, as far as we can understand it, is that of a self-acting power or force —a force with a will within it, and full of attractions and repulsions for the objects around it. It is among these felt attractions or repulsions that the self-moving mind finds its motives. Without motive there is no will; without will no attention; without attention no perception or intelligence. The striking clock may sound as loud as ever in the portal of the ear, and the passing object may paint its image as clear as light in the open eye, but the absorbed and inattentive mind hears no voice and sees no vision. What reader has not sometime read a whole page with the eyes, and when he reached the bottom found himself unable to recall a single word or idea it contained? The sense had done its work, but the mind had been busy with other thoughts.

12. The vigor of mental action, like that of muscular action, is proportioned to the feeling which inspires it. The powers of the intellect do not come forth in their full strength at the mere command of a teacher, nor on the call of some cold sense of duty. Nor can the mind exert its full force upon themes which but lightly touch the feelings. It is only when we "work with a will," that is, with a keen and stirring interest in our work, that we bring our faculties of body or mind out in

their fullest energy. Great occasions make men great. Unsuspected reserve powers come forth as soon as the demand is large enough. In the heat of a great battle, common men become heroic, and weak men strong. So, with deepening interest, attention deepens, and the mind's reserve powers come into work.

SOURCES OF INTEREST

13. The sources of interest, which are the approaches to the attention, are as numerous as the faculties and desires of man and the different aspects of the subjects to be studied. Each organ of sense is the gateway to the pupil's mind, though these gateways differ much in the ease of approach and in the volume and variety of ideas admitted. The hand explores a field limited each moment by the reach of the arm, and takes in only the tactual qualities of matter; but the eye admits the visible universe to its portals with the swiftness of light, and takes note of all of its phenomena of form, size, color, and motion. To command all these gateways of the senses is ordinarily to control the mind. Infants in the cradle may be lured to attention by a bit of bright ribbon, and they will cease feeding or crying to gaze upon some strange object swung before their eyes. The orator's gesturing hand, his smiling or passion-laden look, and his many-toned voice—all mere addresses to the senses—often do more to wake the minds and hold the attention of his auditors than all the meanings of his

speech. The mind cannot refuse to heed that which appeals with power to the senses. Whatever is novel and curious, beautiful, grand, or sublime in mass or motion; whatever is brilliant, strange, or charming in color or combination—the eye fastens and feeds upon these, and the mind comes at its bidding to enjoy and protract the feast.

14. The teacher has not the orator's opportunity for free and grand gesticulation, nor for his commanding use of the voice; but within narrower limits and in finer, because more easy and familiar, play, he has within his power all that face, voice, or hand can do to arrest attention; and has, besides, all that nature and art can afford to address the senses and awaken the intelligence. A sudden pause, with lifted hand, as if listening, will silence all noise in the class and put the pupils to listening also. The sudden showing of a picture, or of some object illustrating the lesson, will attract the most careless and awaken the most apathetic. It is the shock of change, as well as the novelty of a new sensation, which helps to produce the effect. The sudden raising or dropping of the voice arouses fresh attention, as also does a quick and unusual movement of the hands, head, or body. A person who has fallen asleep amid noise wakes when the noise suddenly ceases. The shock of silence awakens the senses put to sleep by monotonous sounds. So, on the contrary, the shock of sudden noise awakens those who are sleeping amid silence.

EFFECT OF A NEW IDEA

15. The influence of shock extends also to the mind. A sudden appeal made to any mental faculty awakens us like the sudden shaking of a sleeper by the shoulder. It drives away all dreaminess and apathy. When we see a careless and listless pupil suddenly become alert and attentive, we say to ourselves: "He has been *struck* with a new idea." He rouses like one who has felt a blow. The shock of a new thought has sometimes had the power to change the entire course of a life, as in the story of the Prodigal Son, and as in less degree all lives change with the changes of thinking.

QUESTIONS THAT STARTLE

16. The awakening and stirring power of a skillful question lies largely in this principle of the shock. It startles the intelligence as with an impinging blow. The ordinary questions read from the book, where the pupils have already seen and answered them, may have their uses, but they lack all power to startle and stir the mind. They simply call for the repetition of thoughts already studied and known. To produce its highest effect, the question must have the element of the unexpected in it. It must surprise the mind with some fresh and novel view of the subject, and must call sharply for new thought. The common style of Sunday-school questions asked with the book open before the pupil, such as: "What did Nicodemus say to Jesus? What did Jesus answer?" has little

power to stir or teach. The mind feels no shake of the shoulder—no stimulating call to wakeful effort. They are sham questions—questions in form only, asking for what is well known and in plain sight. The true question implies the uncertain. It asks for the unseen and unknown. Like bugle blasts, such questions summon all the faculties into the field of action.

THE MENTAL APPETITES

17. Passing within to the field of the mind's own powers, other sources of interest and springs of attention appear. There lurks the imagination ready to take wing with delight at any picturesque, beautiful, or sublime aspect which the lesson may present. There sits the intelligence quick to stir, with its intense curiosity to see and know the hidden and unknown; and there stands the reason, restless till it shall array its facts, construct its theories, collect proofs, and demonstrate its solutions of the problems and questions which the lesson involves. These are the mental appetites, and each has its objects of search, its joy in action, and its pride of achievement.

18. Another source of genuine interest may be found in the connection of the lesson with something in the past life and studies of the learner; and a still richer one in its relations to his future duties and employments. We may add to these the sympathetic interest inspired by the teacher's manifested delight in the theme, and by the generous emulation of fellow

learners in the same field. All these touch the pupil's person-
ality. They appeal to his selfhood. They stir the hopes or fears,
which are quick to color every truth with some bright promise
of good to be gained or shade it with some menace of evil to be
escaped. The mind will brave and undergo the most fatiguing
efforts, and persistently study the most tiresome lessons, to
secure some high advantage or to avoid some threatened
trouble. Self-love, the strongest and most persistent of human
feelings, sways the scepter of a monarch over all faculties and
feelings. When it bids, they wake and work with sharpest
energies. Such are the great sources of the mind's interest in its
objects, and when the appeal can be made to several of them
the effect is deep and intense. The teacher who knows how to
touch all these keys whose vibrant chords thrill mind and heart
may command all the resources of his pupil's soul. But he
should note that any one element of interest felt in its greatest
fullness may be stronger than several only partly awakened.

INTEREST VARIES WITH AGE

19. The sources of interest vary with the ages of learners
and with the advancing stages of growth and intelligence. This
fact is important. The child of six feels little interest and gives
no genuine attention to many of the themes which engross the
mind of the youth of sixteen. In general, the lower motives are
felt first; the nobler and finer come only with years and
culture. The animal appetites awaken long before the

spiritual. Children and adults are often indeed interested in the same scenes and objects, but it does not follow that they are interested in the same ideas. The child finds in the object some striking fact of sense or some personal gratification; the adult mind attends to the profounder relations, the causes or consequences of the fact. As attention follows interest, it is folly to attempt to gain attention to a lesson in which the pupil cannot be led to feel any genuine interest. The assertion that children ought to be compelled to pay attention because it is their duty denies the fundamental condition of attention. If the duty is felt by the child, it is an element of interest; but if it is felt simply in the teacher's mind it only repels. In the little child, affection and sympathy take, in part, the place of conscience, and through these he may be made to feel the claims of obligations which he cannot fully understand. The mother's horror of wrongdoing and her delight in well-doing are felt through sympathy in the heart of her boy; and so, too, the little pupil may be led to feel an interest in studies which the teacher loves and praises, before his intelligence has come to fully appreciate their importance.

20. The power of attention increases with the mental development, and is proportioned nearly to the years of the child. It is one of the most valuable products of education. Idiots and infants are almost destitute of it; even short lessons wearying and exhausting the attention of young children. "Little and often" is the rule for teaching very young pupils.

The power of steady and prolonged attention belongs only to strong minds, and to those trained by long education. Said a man of noted intellectual distinction: "The difference between me and ordinary men lies in my ability to maintain my attention—to keep on plodding."

21. Attention is not a separate faculty of the mind, but rather an active attitude of some or all the faculties. Its power, therefore, must depend upon the number and strength of the faculties involved. Attention will be steadiest when the appeal is made to the strongest faculty. One person can give steady attention to objects of sense, another to objects of the imagination, and a third to processes of reason. A lawyer reads and remembers law cases with great facility; a physician is at once interested in the reports of medical cases, and a clergyman in a new treatise on theology. These are fruits of education; but there are also native diversities of tastes and powers which appear even in childhood. Krüsi,[1] the pupil of Pestalozzi, and himself one of the noblest and most sagacious of teachers, tells of two children. The one, six years old, "sees God every where as an omnipresent man before him. God gives the birds their food; God has a thousand hands; God sits upon all the trees and flowers." The other child, he says, "has an entirely different view of God. To him He is a being afar off, but who from afar sees, hears, and controls everything." So differently

---

[1] Krüsi, Hermann (1775–1844), authority on the object method of teaching. He was an assistant to and then the colleague of Johann Heinrich Pestalozzi.

do the minds of children work. One student is successful in mathematics, another in history, a third in language. To teach in the line of the strongest faculties is to teach with the highest success. Nature itself favors such teaching.

HINDRANCES TO ATTENTION

22. The two chief hindrances to attention are *apathy* and *distraction.* The former may arise from constitutional inertness, from lack of taste for the subject under consideration, or from weariness or other unfavorable bodily condition of the hour. Distraction is the division of the attention between several objects. It is the common fault of undisciplined minds, and is the foe of all sound learning. The quick senses of children are caught so easily by a great variety of objects, and they find in each so little to interest them, that their thoughts flit as with the tireless wing of the butterfly. Memory holds with loose grasp the lessons learned with apathy or distraction, and the reason refuses such poor materials for its work. If the apathy or distraction come from fatigue or illness, the wise teacher will not attempt to force the lesson. Better to let it go for the time, and cheer and lift up the pupil by a kindly sympathy, diverting and arousing him by some unexpected talk or story, or leaving him to rest in quiet.

Rules for Teachers

Out of this Law of the Learner, thus expounded, emerge some of the most important rules for teaching:

1.   Never begin a class exercise till the attention of the class is secured. Study for a moment in silence, the face of each pupil to see if all are mentally, as well as bodily, present.

2.   Pause whenever the attention is interrupted or lost, and wait till it is completely regained.

3.   Never exhaust wholly the pupil's power of attention. Stop when signs of weariness appear, and either dismiss the class or change the subject to kindle fresh attention.

4.   Fit the length of the exercise to the ages of the class: the younger the pupils the briefer the lesson.

5.   Arouse, and when needful rest, the attention by a pleasing variety, but avoid distraction. Keep the real lesson in view.

6.   Kindle and maintain the highest possible interest in the subject itself. Interest and attention react upon each other.

7.   Present those aspects of the lesson, and use such illustrations, as fit the ages, characters, and attainments of the class.

8.   Watch to learn the tastes and strongest faculties of each pupil, and as far as possible address the questions to those tastes and faculties. To do this is to hold the very heartstrings of the pupil.

9.   Find out the favorite stories, songs, and subjects of

each scholar. In these will be found the keys to their mental powers and habits and the ready means to arouse their interest and attention.

10. Watch keenly against all sources of distraction, such as unusual noises and sights, inside the class and out; all contacts and motions discomforting or diverting.

11. Prepare beforehand some questions which will awaken thought, but not beyond the powers and knowledge of the pupils.

12. Address the instruction to as many of the senses and faculties as possible, but beware of drawing the attention from the subject to some mere illustration.

13. Let the teacher maintain in himself and exhibit the closest attention and the most genuine interest in the lesson. True enthusiasm is contagious.

14. Study the best use of the eye and hand. These are the natural instruments of mental command. No pupil can help feeling the earnest gaze fixed upon his face; and none will fail to watch and interpret the lifted hand, the working fingers, the clenched fist, or any of the eloquent movements of these five-fingered monitors.

VIOLATIONS AND MISTAKES

The violations of the Law of the Learner are many, and they constitute the most fatal class of errors committed by ordinary teachers.

(1) Lessons are commenced before the attention of the class is gained, and continued after it has ceased to be given. As well begin before the pupils have entered the room, or continue after they have left. You cannot pour water into a jug while the stopper is in place, nor get sight from the eye when the lids are closed.

(2) Pupils are urged to listen and learn after their limited power of attention is exhausted and when weariness has sealed their minds against any further impression. I remember seeing a teacher of good reputation try to teach a large class the use of the possessive case. She began with all eyes fixed upon her; but, as she went on, one after another lost interest and ceased to attend, till, at the close of her explanation, only one pupil was carefully following, and to this one she addressed her closing question.

(3) Little or no effort is made to discover the tastes of the pupil or to create a real interest in the subject studied. The teacher, feeling no fresh interest in his work, seeks to compel the attention he is unable to attract, and awakens disgust by his dullness and dryness where he ought to inspire delight by his intelligence and active sympathy.

(4) Not a few teachers nearly kill the power of attention in their pupils by neglecting to call it out and give it vigorous exercise. They drone on through dull hours and dreary routine, reading commonplace questions from the

books, without a single fresh inquiry or startling and interesting statement; and without any keen and stirring demand for all the powers of the pupils to rush to action. The children in such schools seek some attitude of lazy ease as soon as they enter the room.

What wonder that through these and other violations of this law of teaching our schools are often made unattractive, and their success is so limited and poor! If obedience to these rules is so important in the common schools, where the attendance of the children is compelled by parents, and where the professional instructor teaches with full authority of law, how much more is it necessary in the Sunday school, where attendance and teaching are voluntary, and where attraction must do the work of authority! Fortunately the Sunday school holds, in the interest of its associations, in the surpassing sacredness and divine grandeur of its themes, in the variety and splendor of its truths and facts, and, above all, in the tender and immortal relationship which these truths establish between the Christian teacher and his pupils, advantages which may amply compensate for the lack of the authority and of the professional experience of the common school. But let the Sunday school teacher who would win the richest and best results of teaching give to this Law of the Learner his profoundest thought and his most patient following. Let him master the art of gaining and keeping attention, and of exciting genuine and stirring interest, and he will wonder and rejoice at the fruitfulness of his work.

IV

THE LAW OF THE LANGUAGE

1. We have now, confronting each other, the Teacher with his law of knowledge, and the Learner with his condition of interested attention. We are next to study the medium of communication between them and learn the Law of the Language.

2. Two minds, housed in material bodies which are at once limiting prisons and living machinery, are to be brought into intellectual intercourse—the fine commerce of thought and feeling. Whatever souls may do in other worlds, in this they have no known spirit connections. Here the organs of sense are parts of material bodies, and can be touched and impressed only by matter and material phenomena. The two minds must find in these physical phenomena the means of intercourse. Out of these they must construct the symbols and

signs by which they can signal to each other the mental facts which they wish to communicate. A system of such symbols or signs is language. It may consist of the picture-writing of the savage races, the alphabets of civilized peoples, the finger alphabet or signs of the deaf-mutes, the oral speech of the hearing, or of the objects of sense, pictures, and gestures; but, whatever its form, or to whatever sense it is addressed, it is language—a medium of communication between minds, a necessary instrument of teaching, and having, like all other factors in the teaching art, its own natural law.

3.   This law, like those already discussed, is as simple as an everyday fact. It may be stated as follows:

The language used in teaching must be common to teacher and learner.

In other words, it must be a true language to each—to him that hears as well as to him that speaks—with the same meaning to both, clear in sense and clearly understood.

THE PHILOSOPHY OF THE LAW

4.   This Law of Language reaches down into the deepest facts of mind, and runs out to the widest connections of thought with life and with the world we live in. The very power of thought rests largely upon this fabric of speech.

5.   Language in its simplest definition is a system of artificial signs. Its separate words have no likeness to the things they signify, and no meanings except those we give them. A

word is the sign of an idea to him alone who has the idea, and who has learned the word as its sign or symbol. Without the idea in the mind, the word comes to the ear only as an unmeaning sound, a sign of nothing at all. No one has more language than he has learned, and the acquisition of a large vocabulary is the work of a lifetime. A teacher may know ten thousand words; the child will scarcely know as many hundreds, but these few hundreds of words represent the child's ideas, and within this narrow circuit of signs and thoughts the teacher must come if he would be understood. Outside of these the teacher's language is as unmeaning to the child as if it were mere drum-taps. His language may sometimes be partially and vaguely understood by reason of the known words scattered through it but may as frequently mislead as lead aright.

6. Most words have more than one meaning. In the common expressions—"Mind and *matter*," "What is the *matter?*" "What *matters* it?" "It is a serious *matter*," "The subject *matter*"—the same word is made not only to carry double, but quadruple. This variety of meanings given to our words may enrich them for the orator and poet, but it is a serious defect in language for the young learner. Having mastered a word as the sign of a familiar idea, he is suddenly confronted by it with a new and unknown meaning. He has learned, perhaps, to fasten a horse to a post, when he hears the strange text, "My days are swifter than a post," or reads the

warning, "Post no bills here," and hears of a "military post." The teacher knowing all the meanings of his words, and guided by the context in selecting the one required by the thought, reads on or talks on, thinking that his language is rich in ideas and bright with intelligence; but his pupils, knowing only a single meaning perhaps for each word, are stopped by great gaps in the sense, bridged only by unmeaning sounds which puzzle and confuse them. It would often amuse us if we could know what ideas our words call up in little children. The boy who wanted to see "the wicked *flea* whom no man pursueth," and the other who said: "Don't view me with a *cricket's* eye," have many classmates in the schools.

THE VEHICLE OF THOUGHT

7.   Language has been called the *vehicle* of thought; but it does not carry thoughts as carts carry goods, to fill an empty storehouse. It rather conveys them as the wires convey telegrams, as signals to the receiving operator, who must retranslate the message from the ticks he hears. Not what the speaker expresses from his own mind, but what the hearer understands and reproduces in *his* mind, measures the exact communicating power of the language used. Words that are poor and weak to the young and ignorant are eloquent with a hundred rich and impressive meanings to the educated and intelligent. Thus the simple word *art* to the common mind means craft—a mechanic's trade or a hypocrite's pretense; to

a Reynolds[1] or a Ruskin[2] it is also the expression of all that is grand and beautiful in human achievement and of all that is benign and elevating in civilization. It speaks of paintings, sculptures, and cathedrals, and of all that is beautiful in nature, in landscape, sky, and sea—all that is noble or picturesque in history and life—all that is hidden in the moral and aesthetic nature of man. Men's words are ships freighted with the riches of every shore of knowledge which their owner has visited; a child's words are but toy boats on which are loosely loaded the simple notions he has picked up in his playgrounds.

8.   So, too, words come often to be loved or hated for the ideas they suggest. Thus the word *religion*, to the Christian thinker, is sacred and sublime with the divinest meanings. It paints on the dark background of human history, filled with sin and sorrow, all that is glorious in the character and government of God, all that is highest in faith and feeling, and all that is hopeful and bright in the immortality of man. To the mere worldling it is the name of a mass of disagreeable ceremonies or of more distasteful duties. To the atheist it is the expression of what he calls degrading superstitions and hateful creeds. In a less marked degree, such variations of significance belong to hundreds of the common words of our language. It is evident that he will teach most and best whose well-chosen words

[1] Reynolds, Sir Joshua (1723–1792), English portrait painter and aesthetitian.
[2] Ruskin, John (1819-1900), lauded English art critic and social commentator.

raise the most and clearest images, and excite the highest action, in the minds of his pupils.

9. The reason goes further. In all true teaching thought passes in both directions—from pupil to teacher as well as from teacher to pupil. It is as needful that the man shall clearly understand the child as it is that the child shall understand the man. A child often loads a common word with some strange, false, or half meaning, and years may pass before the mistake is detected and corrected. Their very poverty of speech often compels children to use words out of the true sense. How shall the teacher know what to teach till he knows what the pupil needs to learn? And how shall he know the pupil's needs till he learns it from that pupil's words?

THE INSTRUMENT OF THOUGHT

10. But language is the *instrument,* as well as the vehicle, of thought. Words are tools under whose plastic touch the mind reduces the crude masses of its impressions into clear and valid propositions. Ideas become incarnate in words. They rise into visible forms in language, and stand ready to be studied and known, to be marshaled into the combinations and mechanism of intelligible thought. Till our conceptions are thus shaped into expression, they flit as vague phantoms, intangible and indistinct. Their real character and value, and their manifold and useful relations, are unknown, if not also unsuspected. More than half the work of teaching is that of

helping the child to gain a full and clear expression of what it already knows imperfectly. It is to aid him to lift up into full sight, and to round out into plain and adequate sentences, the dim and fragmentary ideas and perceptions of childhood. No teaching is complete that does not issue in plain and intelligent expression of the truth taught; but it is the most miserable of mockeries when, in place of leading the child to perfect and put into its own simple speech its own simple conceptions of truth, we impose upon it the ready-made definitions of some learned master or teacher, dressed, for the most part, in words it never heard before. Better David's simple sling than Saul's kingly armor for the young warrior seeking the mastery over some science.

11. We may go further, and say that in a large degree talking is thinking. Ideas must precede words in all but parrot speech. The most useful, and sometimes the most difficult, processes in thinking are those in which we fit words to ideas, and fashion sentences to express thoughts. To state a question or problem fully and clearly is often the best part of answering it. Ideas rise before us at first like the confused mass of objects in a new landscape. To put them into clear and correct words and sentences is to make the landscape familiar.

"Thoughts disentangle passing o'er the lip."

12. We master truth by expressing it, and rejoice when we have clearly expressed our thought as one who has gained a victory. But to make talking thinking it must be original, not

mere parrot-like repetition of other people's words. In this battle with truth, reluctant to surrender itself, it is the child's own hand that must grasp and use the weapon. It is the pupil who must talk. What teacher has not stood and watched the battle when a little group of children have attacked some knotty problem, and each in turn has tried to reduce the truth to proper speech? and how proud and honored the victor when he has forced the thought into the fitting words which all recognized as the true expression! Krüsi tells of one of his pupils who was set to write a letter to his parents, and complained: "It is hard for me to write a letter." "Why! you are now a year older, and ought to be better able to do it." "Yes; but a year ago I could say everything I knew, but now I know more than I can say." Krüsi adds: "This answer astonished me." It will astonish all who have not thought deeply of the difficulty of getting a mastery of language to express our thoughts.

13. Language has yet another use. It is the *storehouse* of our knowledge. All that we know of any object, fact, or truth may be found laid up in the words we use concerning them. Words are not only the signs of our ideas, but they are clue lines by which we recover and recognize those ideas at will, and in the manifold derivative forms and combinations of these words we store up all the modifications and relations of the radical fact or notion of which the simple word is the symbol. In the group or family of words, act, acted, acting, actor, actress, action, actionable, active, actively, activity, actual,

actually, actualize, actuality, actuate, enact, exact, transact, and the derivatives of these last forms what a volume of facts and truths—of persons, movements, relations, qualities, and philosophy lies recorded!

14. The child's language, then, is not only the measure of its knowledge, but is the virtual embodiment of the elements of that knowledge. When we employ in our teaching the language of our pupils, we summon all their acquired intelligence to our aid. Each word flashes its own familiar light upon the new truth we wish to exhibit. The first new and unknown word introduced breaks the electric chain of thought. A shadow falls upon the field of view, and the pupils cease to work or grope in darkness. New words must be learned when new objects are to be named or new ideas are to be symbolized; but if care is taken that the idea shall go before the word, and that the word is mastered as a symbol before it is used in speech, it will illumine and guide where otherwise it would but darken and delude.

THE LANGUAGE OF THINGS

15. Words are not the only medium through which mind speaks to mind. The thinker has a hundred ways to express his thoughts. The eye talks with a various eloquence; and the skilled orator finds in lip and brow, in head and hand, in the shrugging shoulder and the stamping foot, organs for most intelligible speech. The gestures of John B. Gough[3] often tell

[3] John Bartholomew Gough (1817–1886), American temperance orator.

more than the clearest sentences of other speakers. A German described him as "the man what talks mit his coattails," referring to some illustration in which the facile orator had made a flirt of his coattails tell the idea he wished to express. Deaf- mutes can talk together by the hour by signs, without spelling out a single word. Among savage peoples whose language is too meager to meet the native needs of their minds, symbolic actions supply the lack of words. There is also speech in pictures. From the rudest chalk sketch on the blackboard to the highest work of the painter's art, no teaching is more swift and impressive than that of pictorial representation. The eye gathers here at a glance more than the ear could learn from an hour of verbal description.

16. Finally, nature aids human speech. "She speaks a various language."[4] Her innumerable forms stand always ready as illustrations, and her endless analogies throw light upon hundreds of our deepest and darkest problems. No teaching was ever more clear or instructive than that of the parables of Jesus drawn from nature around Him.

17. In ordinary teaching, artificial language must doubtless be the chief means of communication between master and learner; but no wise teacher will forget or forego the aid of all these various means of entrance into the chambers of his pupil's understanding, to take account of the knowledge there, and to guide to the mastery of more. Language is at best an

[4] William Cullen Bryant (1794–1878), "Thanatopsis" (1817).

imperfect medium of thought. None know this better than the experienced teacher who has tried to use it for the conveyance of the higher truths of science or religion, and who has found himself forced to seize upon every available means of illustration to get himself understood.

18. This discussion of language is not to be interpreted as an encouragement to the teacher to become a lecturer before his class. The lecture is useful in its place, but its place is small in a school for children. It will be shown elsewhere that a too talkative teacher is rarely a good teacher. A fine and accurate knowledge of language is still of great use, for he who talks but little should talk well, and he who must teach language should know that which he is to teach.

RULES FOR TEACHERS

Out of our Law of Language, thus defined and explained, flow some of the most useful rules for teaching.

1. Study constantly and carefully the pupil's language to learn what words he uses and the meanings he gives them.

2. Secure from him as full a statement as possible of his knowledge of the subject, to learn both his ideas and his mode of expressing them, and to help him to correct his language.

3. Express your thoughts as far as possible in the pupil's words, carefully correcting any defect in the meaning he gives them.

4. Use the simplest and fewest words that will express the

idea. Unnecessary words add to the child's work and increase the danger of misunderstanding.

5.   Use short sentences, and of the simplest construction. Long sentences tire the attention, while short ones both stimulate and rest the mind. At each step the foot rests firmly on the ground.

6.   If the pupil evidently fails to understand the thought, repeat it in other language and if possible with greater simplicity.

7.   Help out the meaning of the words by all available illustrations; preferring pictures and natural objects for young children.

8.   When it is necessary to teach a new word, give the idea before the word. This is the order of nature.

9.   Seek to increase the pupil's stock of words, both in number and in the clearness and extent of meaning. All true enlargement of a child's language is increase of his knowledge and of his capacity for knowing.

10. As the acquisition of language is one of the most important objects of education, be not content to have the pupils listen in silence, however attentive they may seem. That teacher is succeeding best whose pupils talk most freely upon the lessons.

11.   Here, as everywhere in teaching the young, *make haste slowly.* Let each word be conquered into use before it is displaced by too many others.

12.   Test frequently the pupil's sense of the words he uses,

to make sure that he attaches no false meaning and that he vividly conceives the true meaning.

VIOLATIONS AND MISTAKES

This third law of teaching is violated more frequently than even the best teachers suspect.

(1) The interested look and the smiling assent of the pupil often cheat the teacher into the belief that his language is understood, and all the more easily because the pupil himself is deceived and says he understands, when, in fact, he has caught only a mere glimpse of the meaning.

(2) Children are often entertained with the manner of the teacher, and seem attentive to his words when they are only watching his eyes, lips, or actions. They sometimes profess to understand simply to please their instructor and to gain his praise.

(3) The misuse of language is perhaps one of the most common failures in teaching. Not to mention those pretended teachers who cover up their own ignorance or indolence with a cloud of verbiage which they know the children will not understand, and omitting also those who are more anxious to exhibit their own wisdom than to convey knowledge to others, we find still some honest teachers who labor hard to make the lesson clear, and then feel that their duty is done. If the

children do not understand, it must be from hopeless stupidity or from willful inattention. They do not suspect that they have used words which have no meaning to the class or to which the children give a meaning differing from the teacher's. I once heard a legislator, who was also a preacher, in addressing the pupils of a reform school on the parable of the Prodigal Son, ask the question: "Boys, are you of the opinion that the customary aliments of swine are adapted to the digestive apparatus of the *genus homo?*" An interrogative grunt was the only reply.

(4) It may be a single unusual or misunderstood term that breaks the electric line; but it does not occur to the teacher to hunt up the break and restore the connection. Two adults rarely talk five minutes without having occasion to ask the sense of some word used or a restatement of some thought advanced. But children do not ask explanations. Fear of the teacher, or a sense of their own ignorance, discourages them, and too often they are charged with stupidity or inattention when no amount of attention would have helped them to understand the unknown tongue.

(5) Even those teachers who easily use simple language to their classes frequently fail in the higher use of this instrument of teaching. They do not take care to secure from the child in return a clear statement of the truth,

and they have, therefore, no test of their success. The children do not talk back.

(6) Very few teachers appreciate as they ought the wonderful character and complexity of language, this most magnificent product of the human intelligence, and this mightiest agency of human advancement and influence. Modern society could not exist without speech; and the richest commerce that is carried on among men and nations is that which is freighted in words, "the airy navies of the world." The English language claims over 100,000 words. Few men understand more than 20,000 of these, and the vocabulary of a child of ten rarely contains more than 1500. It has been found that the greatest obstacle to the general enlightenment of the common people lies in their lack of knowledge of the language through which they must be addressed. A commission from the British Parliament was once set to investigate the language of the coalminers and other laborers of England, to ascertain the possibility of diffusing useful information among them by means of tracts and books. It was found, as reported, that their knowledge of language, in a large number of the cases examined, was too meager to allow of such means of instruction. How much greater must be this deficiency among the young, whose experience is less and whose

imperfection of ideas compels vagueness in language! If we would teach children successfully, we must deepen and widen this channel of communication between our minds and theirs.

(7) Most of the topics studied in school lie outside the daily life and language of children; and every science has a language of its own which must be mastered by him who will learn its truths. And if in common science this need of language is so great, how much more in those high, spiritual themes with which the Sunday-school teacher has to deal! Religion involves the grandest facts and the sublimest truths known to the mind of man; but how are they dwarfed and distorted by the half-understood terms in which they are frequently told! The Word of God is the sword of the Spirit; but how shall it make its way to heart and conscience when wrapped in a mass of half-concealing words? To the teacher of children in the schools of Bible learning, more than to any others, should come the warning to make his words clear as plate glass, luminous as light itself, sharp as polished blades, painting truths as "apples of gold in pictures of silver,"[5] and stirring the depths of the mind as the bugle stirs an army.

[5] Proverbs 25:11

V

The Law of the Lesson

1.   Our fourth law takes us at once to the center of the teaching work. The first three laws defined the teacher, the learner, and language, the medium of communication between them. We come now to the Lesson—the truth or fact to be learned, the process to be mastered, or the problem to be solved—the knowledge which the teacher seeks to give and the learner studies to gain. To make the unknown known; to give knowledge to the pupil as a personal possession; to place it as an active force in his mind; to plant it as an inspiring principle in his heart; to kindle it as a guiding light in his understanding; to make it to him a growing germ of higher knowledge, an instrument of research, a practical power in his life and work— this is the very core of the teacher's work, the condition and instrument, as well as the crown and fruitage, of all the rest.

2.   It is the Law of the Lesson, or of knowledge, we are next to seek. Passing, as too remote, all discussion of the steps by which an infant mind obtains its first ideas, and of the mental processes by which our sensations ripen into true perceptions, and these into reflective knowledge, we go at once to the obvious fact that our pupils learn new truths by the aid of those that are old and familiar. The new and unknown can be explained only by the familiar and the known. This, then, is the Law of the Lesson:

The truth to be taught must be learned through truth already known.

3.   This law is neither so simple nor so obvious as those which have preceded it; but it is no less certain than they, while its scope is wider and its relations are more important. It lies linked with the great system of nature and with the constitution of the mind.

TRUTH, IDEAL AND ACTUAL

4.   Truth in its entirety is but the ideal transcript of the universe. It is the mirrored reflection of all fact and being—the thought and will of the Creator as written and revealed by all that exists, material and spiritual, with all their laws, relations, changes, evolutions, and history. More—the alltruth embraces the being of God Himself.

Truth in actions, in art, in objects, in conduct, and in character is only the correlative of truth in ideas; it is the conformity of the actual to the true ideal—the fact answering to the divine law and purpose of things. Truth in action—that is wisdom, that is the Right and the Good.

THE KNOWN AND UNKNOWN

5.   Knowledge is truth discovered and understood. Truth yet hidden in the depths and ocean of the undiscovered is the Unknown. The Known is science, learning—the revealed. It is the gold taken from the mines of truth by human hands and wrought into forms of beauty or of use, or coined into currency for the markets of the world. The Unknown is the precious metal lying hidden under sea and land, seen only by Omniscience. The Known, to each individual, is that truth which he has mastered and made his own; all else is to him the Unknown. Much which is to the teacher knowledge is to the child the Unknown, and it is to this Unknown that our law especially applies. The path of learning to this must be constructed through the pupil's knowledge.

PHILOSOPHY OF THE LAW

6.   The Law of the Lesson has its reason in the nature of mind and the nature of human knowledge.

7.   All teaching must begin at some point of the subject or lesson. Where can it begin but at that which is seen or known by the learner? If the subject is wholly new, or the fact to be taught is entirely strange, then a known point must be sought

or made by showing some likeness of the new and unknown to something known and familiar. Even among grown people the skillful converser, narrating a new fact, struggles to find some comparison with familiar objects, and affirms some likeness of the unknown to a known thing before proceeding with his description or story. Till this starting point in the familiar is found, he knows it is useless to go on. As well bid one to follow you through a winding way in the pitch darkness without first letting him know where you are or putting him in the path. If intelligent men require this known starting-point in some familiar fact or truth, how shall the child be expected to proceed without it? How often and how justly do children explain their seeming stupidity by the simple statement: "I did not know what the teacher was talking about"! It is the teacher, and not the pupil, who is stupid in such a case.

8. All teaching must advance in some direction. Whitherward shall it march but to that which is to the pupil new and unknown? To teach again what is already known and understood is to mock the pupil's desire for knowledge, and to deaden his power of attention by compelling him to walk the weary round of a treadmill, in place of leading him forward to the inspiration of new scenes and the conquest of new truths. No more fatal blow can be dealt to a child's native love of learning than to confine its studies too long to familiar ground under the fallacious plea of thoroughness. Old mines may be reworked if you can find ore at deeper levels, and old lessons

may be relearned if new truth can be dug out or new uses made of old truth. Properly understood, this does not contradict the law of the review, to be discussed in another chapter.

9.   All learning must proceed by some steps. By what steps can it advance except by those which link one fact or truth to another, as simple facts lead to more general facts, premises conduct to conclusions, and phenomena come at last to the explaining laws and reasons? In all true learning, each new fact mastered becomes a part of the known, and serves as a new starting-point for a fresh advance. It adds its own light to the knowledge that preceded it, and throws increased illumination forward for the next discovery. But each step must be fully mastered before taking the next, else at the second step the pupil will be moving from the unknown to the unknown, and thus violate the law. It is here that the demand for true thoroughness arises; not the thorough mastery which a philosopher might gain of the lesson and all it contains, but such a clear understanding as the child may have of so much of the lesson as a child can comprehend. Thoroughness of this sort is the essential condition of true teaching. Imperfect knowledge at any point casts shadow rather than light. The half-known reveals nothing. It is simply disturbed ignorance, and soon settles again into complete ignorance. The pupil who knows thoroughly one lesson, already half knows the next. The known explains the nearest unknown, as the lighted torch drives back darkness. Hence

the well-taught class is eager for the next lesson. They guess already the coming truth. "It is easy to add to what is already discovered." This was one of the sayings of Pestalozzi.

10. But the philosophy of this law goes deeper still. Knowledge is not a mass of simple independent facts revealed to the senses; it is made up of facts with their laws and relations. Facts stand linked together in classes, groups, and systems; associated by likeness, by causation, by contact and environment. Each fact is related to innumerable other facts; each truth is a part of some larger truth which includes and explains it. The truths and facts known are but the seen segments of the all-fact and all-truth whose grander segments are still hidden in the vast unknown. Knowledges are mutually illustrative. Each one leads to, and explains, another. The old reveals the new; the new confirms and corrects the old.

11. All this is as true of children's knowledge as of riper and larger sciences. Every new fact or truth must be brought into connection or comparison with facts and truths already known before it will fully reveal itself and take its place in the widening circle of knowledge. Thus the very nature of knowledge compels us to seek the unknown through the aid of the known. To know one thing, we must know many. To know that an object is a flower, the child must know other flowers; to know it as a rose he must know other roses; to know its petals, calyxes, stamens, and pistils, and their uses, he must know these organs in other plants. And so of all other objects of sense. And so also in a

higher degree of the objects of the spiritual sense, the facts of mind, of conscience, and of affection. It is the law of all knowledge whatever. It is probable that this discussion itself will seem to some readers dull, obscure, and of little interest or importance simply from their lack of knowledge of the mental phenomena and science necessary to understand the statements and principles here involved.

12. The very act of knowing is an act of comparing and judging, and one of the terms under comparison always belongs to the known. We have no mental power by which we can gain knowledge otherwise. Even the eye—that openest of all the avenues of intelligence—comes under the same condition. Every object when first seen is strange and nondescript. It begins to be known when we find in it some resemblance to an object before known, and then we pronounce it a stick or a stone, or whatever its recognized likeness reveals it to be, and we know it better as we detect by fuller comparison more resemblances. If a friend tells us an experience or an adventure, we interpret his story by a running comparison of it with whatever has been most like it in our own experience; and if he states facts utterly without likeness to all we have known, we stop him to ask explanations or illustrations which may bring the strange facts into connection with our knowledge of things. Tell a child something utterly novel and differing entirely from all his former experience and knowledge, and he will struggle in vain

to understand you. If he does not at once abandon the effort as hopeless, he eagerly asks: "What is it like? How does it look?" and thus seeks instinctively to bring it under the light of facts already known to him. The whole system of figures of speech—tropes, metaphors, similes, comparisons, parables, and illustrative stories—has sprung out of this law. They are but so many attempts to reach the unknown through the known—they seek to flash some light from the familiar and well-known upon the strange or halfknown.

THE UNKNOWN CANNOT EXPLAIN THE UNKNOWN

13. It is evident that the unknown cannot be explained by the unknown. The very notion of explanation is the citation and use of facts or principles already familiar, to make clear the nature of new facts. The knowledge already possessed must furnish the explanation of all new facts and phenomena, or they must remain unexplained. The difficulty so often felt in answering the questions of little children lies not so much in the hardness of the questions themselves, as in the child's lack of the knowledge required in the explanation. To answer fully a boy's questionings about the stars, you must first teach him astronomy. The lad who has seen a city can easily understand a description of London or Paris, but one whose observation has been confined to his country home cannot picture to himself the interminable network of streets, walled in by blocks of lofty buildings with all the shifting panorama of life and traffic.

14. The very language with which new knowledge must be expressed takes all its meanings from old knowledge. The child without knowledge would be also without words, for words are but signs of things known—of our ideas or notions of things known to us. An American traveler in Europe fancied he could make people understand him by speaking with a loud, clear, and slow pronunciation, forgetting for the moment that his words had no meaning whatever to his listeners. Similar is the blunder of the teacher who hopes by the mere urgency of his manner, and by his clear use of words familiar to himself, to carry his ideas into the very center of the pupil's understanding without any reference to that pupil's previous knowledge of the subject. He violates a law of nature as inflexible as that which forbids vision without light, hearing without sound, or feeling without touch.

15. The mind uses by preference only its clearest and most familiar knowledge in the interpretation of new facts. Each man borrows his illustrations from his calling: the soldier from the camps and marches, the sailor from the ships and the sea, the merchant from the market, and the artisan from his craft. And so in the objects of study, each student is attracted to the qualities which relate it to his business or experience. To the chemist, common salt is chloride of sodium, a binary compound; to the cook it is a condiment used to season food and preserve meats. Each thinks of it in the aspect most familiar to him, and in this aspect would use it to

illustrate any other truth. Finding a new plant, the botanist would compare it with known plants, to discover its class and species; the farmer would ask after its use, and the painter after its beauty. This bent of preference is one of the elements of prejudice which shuts the eyes to some truths and opens them wide to others. It is also one of *the* elements of strength in intellectual work.

16. A fact or truth only partly and imperfectly known is used rarely and reluctantly as a term in the judgments by which we seek to discover the nature and value of new truth; and if used, it carries its own vagueness and imperfection into the new knowledge. A cloud left upon the lesson of yesterday casts its shadow over the lesson of today. On the other hand, the thoroughly mastered lesson throws its illuminating light over each succeeding one. Hence the value of that practice of some able teachers who make the elementary portions of a new study familiar as household words—a perfectly conquered territory from which the pupil may go on to new conquests as from an established base, with the confidence and power of a victor.

17. But it must be carefully noted that such a conquest of elements, like all thoroughness in study, is relative. No human knowledge is perfect, and the knowledge of childhood is necessarily less complete than that of manhood. What would be thoroughness in a child would be but shallowness in a man; and there are wide differences between men. The

thought-pictures of one are but sketches in outline; those of another are paintings in colors, full of light and shades minutely representing nature itself. Young teachers, urged on by the constant exhortations to thoroughness given them by older educators, and not reflecting that a child's knowledge is necessarily less than that of grown men, attempt to hold their little pupils to each lesson studied till they know it with the same fullness as the teacher himself. As well ask the child to walk with a man's stride and speak with a man's voice. What is wanted is not absolute completeness of knowledge as the book may give it, but clear and correct thinking and knowing up to the limits within which the child can know—such knowledge as the pupil's previous knowledge has made possible, and such as will serve him to learn more. He who knows little can learn little; he who knows much can easily learn much. "To him that hath shall be given, and he shall have abundantly. From him that hath not shall be taken away that which he seemeth to have."[1]

RULES FOR TEACHERS

This law of knowledge, written thus in the very nature of truth, as also in the nature of mind, and having therefore a double testimony to its verity and importance, affords to the thoughtful teacher rules of the highest practical value. Marking the sole possible pathway to knowledge, it offers a

[1] Matthew 13:12

clue of clearest guidance to him who will unyieldingly follow it. The following rules seem self-evident:

1.   Find what your pupil knows of the subject you wish to teach—not of some textbook, but of the facts and elements of the subject. This is his starting point.

2.   Make the most of the pupil's knowledge. Let him feel its extent and value as a means of learning more.

3.   Lead him to clear up and freshen his knowledge by attempting a clear statement of it. This will bring him to the border of the unknown.

4.   Begin with facts which lie next, and which can be reached by a single step from those already familiar— geography with the visible landscape, or some river or mountain the pupil has visited—history, with his own memories—morals, with his own conscience.

5.   Connect every lesson as much as possible with former lessons, and with the pupil's knowledge and experience.

6.   Study the steps so that one shall lead naturally and easily to the next, the known leading to the unknown.

7.   Proportion the steps to the age and power of the pupil, and make sure that he understands fully the new truth. Each additional fact, reason, proof, and inference may be treated as a step. Do not discourage the little one with too long lessons, nor disgust older pupils with lessons too short and easy.

8.   Find illustrations in the most common and familiar objects and facts suitable for the purpose. They will carry their

own familiarity into the subject.

9.   Lead the pupil to find fresh illustrations of the lesson in something he has seen or heard.

10. Make every new truth familiar and fix it in the memory for ready use to explain other truths.

11. Incite the pupil to use his knowledge in all ways practicable, to find or explain other knowledge. Teach him that knowledge gives power to know more; that the known is the key to the unknown.

12. Make every advance clear and familiar, else the next step may be from unknown to unknown—a violation of the law.

These rules apply to all kinds of learning: to arithmetic, grammar, geography, history, and to both scientific and religious knowledge; but the teacher, to apply them wisely, must understand the nature of the knowledge he would teach. Science, history, philosophy, language, and religion, each has its own kind of facts, its own method of proof, and its own law of acquisition and use. Science is learned chiefly through the senses or by observation; history is human experience; philosophy is the work of reason; language represents the forms of thought; religion belongs to the conscience, the heart, the faith in the eternal and the divine. But whatever the kind of truth, be it science or Scripture, the unknown must be reached through the known. Some experience may be required to apply these rules readily; but the very effort to use them will reveal to the observant teacher some of the richest secrets of the teacher's art.

MISTAKES AND VIOLATIONS

The wide scope and profound reach of this great Law of the Lesson affords room for many mistakes and violations. Among the more common are the following:

1. Setting young pupils to study strange lessons or new subjects for which they have had no preparation in previous life or studies.

2. The neglect to ascertain with care the pupil's knowledge of the subject before beginning the advance.

3. The failure to connect the new lesson with the old in such a way that the pupil shall bring forward what he knows to explain the new. Lessons are too often given haphazard and treated as if each were independent of all others.

4. Treating past acquisitions like goods finished and stored away, not recognizing that the knowledge gained is the very instrument of fresh learning.

5. The common failure to make thoroughly familiar the elementary facts and definitions.

6. The like failure to make each step thoroughly understood before taking the next.

7. The frequent assignment of lessons too long for the power or time of the pupil, compelling him to imperfect knowledge, which hinders and spoils all after-progress, making the pupil feel as if dragged at a cart-tail rather than as walking erect on his own feet.

8.   The neglect to set the child to the use of his knowledge to become a discoverer of new truth.

9.   The failure to show the connections of knowledge, new and old, and especially with the unknown sought for.

As a consequence of these and other violations of this law, how poor, fragmentary, and fleeting is much of the knowledge so laboriously studied! How little of true knowledge is possessed by the people, and how little their ability to get new knowledge! Instead of temples of truth rising from solid foundations, beautiful in proportions and noble in use, the knowledge of most men lies in little scattered heaps, like those which boys scrape together by the dusty roadside. Such, too often, is the knowledge of Bible truth, made up of scattered texts and bits of exegesis. The sacred volume is never seen by most men as a grand whole, joined together by deep connections and having a single divine and mighty purpose running through it all. Instead of a true revelation of God—a magnificent mirror reflecting His eternal grace and glory—they find in it only bits of broken glass which show the divine will and wisdom in distorted parts, and often puzzle where they should instruct and persuade.

VI

THE LAW OF THE TEACHING PROCESS

1.   Our survey of the teaching art has thus far taken in the four entities involved in an act of teaching: the Teacher, the Learner, the Language, and the Lesson. We are now to contemplate these in motion, and to study the distinctive action of the teacher and his pupil. The previous discussions have already brought these partly into view; but as each of them has its own natural law, each demands a more careful discussion than has yet been given it. In the laws of the teacher and the learner we found necessarily reflected the functions of both; but an actor and his act are easily separated in thought, and each possesses aspects and characteristics of its own.

Following the natural order, the teaching act or function comes first before us, and we are now to seek its law. The law of the teacher was a law of essential qualification. The law of teaching is a law of function.

2.   Thus far we have considered teaching as the communication of knowledge; but this defines the act by its results. Whether by telling, showing, explaining, or setting lessons, the teacher seems to communicate knowledge. But there is a deeper and truer view of the teacher's work, a profounder and more philosophical explanation of his function. Behind and beyond all the telling, explaining, and lesson-giving, there lies as the essential aim of it all, and of all that the teacher does, the awakening and setting in action the learner's mind, the arousing of his self-activities, as they have been called—those faculties of cognition, imagination, and reasoning whose action must always be voluntary and self-impelled. As already shown, knowledge cannot be passed from mind to mind like apples from one basket to another, but must in every case be re-cognized, re-thought by the receiving mind. All telling, explaining, or other acts of so-called teaching are useless except as they serve to excite and direct the pupil's voluntary mental powers. If these are not put in action, nothing follows; the teacher's words fall upon deaf ears.

3.   This may therefore be taken as

The Law of Teaching:
Excite and direct the self-activities of the learner,
and tell him nothing that he can learn himself.

4.   The latter clause is only a limiting caution whose importance is so great as to require its statement as part of the

law. There are cases in which this caution must be disregarded in order to save time, or to favor a weak or discouraged pupil, but its violation is always a loss which should be compensated by some greater gain. Taken in its affirmative form, this caution would read: "Leave the pupil to discover the truth for himself—make him a truth-finder." The validity and value of this law have been too often and too strongly stated to demand further proof. No great writer on education has failed to notice and enunciate it under some form or other; and if we were seeking for the educational maxim the most widely received among good teachers, and the most extensive in its applications and results, we should inevitably fix upon this. It is the truth recognized in such rules as the following, so often urged by eminent teachers upon beginners: "Wake up the mind"; "Set pupils to thinking"; "Arouse the spirit of inquiry"; "Get your pupils to work." All these maxims are but various expressions of one law.

In tracing the laws of attention, of language, and of knowledge, the mental faculties acting under those laws have necessarily come into view, but they will now demand a fuller and more explicit discussion; for it is in the modes of mental action that we must seek the

PHILOSOPHY OF THE LAW.

5. We can learn without a teacher. Children learn hundreds of facts before they are sent to school, sometimes with the aid of parents or others, but often by their own

unaided activities. In the greater part of our acquisitions we are all self-taught, and it is generally conceded that the knowledge is most permanent and best in use which is dug out by unaided research. All knowledge, at the outset, must be learned by its discoverer without an instructor, since no instructor knows it. If, then, we can learn without teaching, it follows that the true and only function of a teacher is to stimulate and help the learner to do what he might otherwise do by himself and without a teacher. Essentially the acquisition of knowledge must be made by the same faculties used in the same methods, whether with or without a teacher.

6. What, then, is the use of schools, and what the necessity of a teacher? The question is pertinent, the answer plain. Knowledge lies in nature in scattered facts, mixed and con- fused; connected, it is true, in great systems, but connected by laws and relations hidden from the tyro's vision, and learned by mankind only through ages of observation. The school selects for its curriculum what it regards as the most useful of nature's truths, and offers these with all the gathered facilities for learning them. It secures to the learner leisure and quiet for study, and offers in its books and apparatus the results of the labors of other learners, which may serve as charts of the territories to be explored, and as beaten paths through the fields of knowledge. True teaching is not that which *gives* knowledge, but that which stimulates pupils to *gain* it. It may be said that *he teaches best who teaches*

least; or, better still, he teaches most whose pupils learn most without his teaching.

7.   The teacher is a sympathizing guide whose familiarity with the subjects to be learned enables him to direct the learner's efforts, to save him from the waste of time and strength, or needless or insuperable difficulties, and to keep him from mistaking truth for error. But no aid of school or teacher can change nature's modes in mind work, or take from the learner the lordly prerogative and need for knowing for himself. The eye must do its own seeing, the ear its own hearing, and the mind its own thinking, however much may be done to furnish objects of sight, sounds for the ear, and ideas for the intelligence. It is the child's own inward digestion which produces growth of body or mind. "If childhood is educated according to the measure of its powers," said St. Augustine, "they will continually grow and increase; while if forced beyond their strength, they decrease instead of increasing."[1] The sooner the teacher abandons the false notion that he can make his pupils intelligent by hard work on their passive receptivity, the sooner he may attain the true teacher's art, as Socrates expressed it, to assist the mind to shape and put forth its own conceptions. It was to his skill in this that the great Athenian[2] owed his power and greatness among his contemporaries, and gave him the place he still holds as next to Jesus of Nazareth, that foremost among the great

[1] St. Augustine (354–430), considered one of the greatest defenders of the true faith, a classical scholar and biblical teacher of the Early Church.
[2] Socrates (470-399 BC), considered the first of the great ancient philosophers.

teachers of mankind. It is the "forcing process" in teaching which separates *learning* from *knowing*. A boy having expressed surprise at the shape of the earth, when he was shown a globe, was asked: "Did you not learn that in school?" he replied: "Yes, I learned it, but I never knew it."

8. The two great coordinate aims of education are to *acquire knowledge* and *to develop power*. Our law derives its significance from both of these aims. The pupil must *know* for himself, or his knowledge will be knowledge only in form. The very effort required in the act of thus learning and knowing gives both vividness to the knowledge learned and increases the power to learn. Mental toil gives to the mind both appetite and digestive power, and he who is taught without study, like him who is fed without exercise, will lose both appetite and strength.

9. But the argument goes deeper. Confidence in our own powers is an essential condition of their successful exercise. This confidence can be gained only by the self-prompted, voluntary, and independent use of these powers. We gain confidence to walk by walking, not by seeing others walk. So the faith we need to feel in our own intellect must come from the self-controlled and successful use of that intellect.

10. The self-activities or voluntary mental powers do not set themselves at work without some motive or excitant to put them in action. They sleep as if behind closed doors till some external object touches the senses or some internal craving or emotion stirs the thought. Of these two classes of excitants, the

external are strongest in early life, the internal in riper years. To the young child the objects of sense—bright colors, live animals, and things in motion—are most attractive and mind-exciting. At the other end of life, the inner facts of thought and feeling most stir and engage the powers. The child's mental life has in it an excess of sensation; the old man's an excess of reflection.

11. But whatever the excitant which starts the mental powers, the processes of cognition are nearly the same. There is the comparison of the new with the old, the alternating analysis and synthesis of parts, wholes, classes, causes, and effects; the reciprocal action of memory and imagination, the combinations of the judgment and the reason, and the various excursions of thought controlled by the tastes, powers, needs, and previous knowledge of each thinker. If this inner and voluntary action does not go on, the teacher has applied his external excitants in vain. He may wonder that he cannot *make* his pupil understand and remember, and will perhaps impatiently believe him stupid and incompetent or idle. The stupidity is often on the other side, and it sins against this plain law of teaching in assuming that the teacher can make the pupil learn by dint of vigorous telling, or teaching as he calls it, whereas true teaching only brings to bear upon the pupil's mind nature's various excitants. If some of these fail, he must find others, and rest not till he reaches the desired result and sees in full play upon the lesson the self-activities of the child.

12. Said Comenius,[3] over two hundred years ago: "Most teachers sow plants instead of seeds of plants; instead of proceeding from the simplest principles, they introduce the scholar at once into a chaos of books and miscellaneous studies." The figure of the seed is a good one, and is much older than Comenius. The greatest of teachers said: "The seed is the word."[4] The true teacher does but stir the ground and sow the seed. It is the work of the soil through its own forces to develop the growth and ripen the grain.

13. The difference between the self-acting pupil and the pupil who only acts when he is acted on is too obvious to need description. The one acts as a living and free agent; the other resembles a machine. The former is attracted by his work, and, prompted by his own inborn interest, he works on till he meets some overcoming difficulty or reaches the end of his task. The latter moves only as he is moved upon. He sees what is shown him, hears what is told, advances when the teacher leads, and stops just where and when the teaching stops. The one moves by self-activities, the other by a borrowed impulse. The former is a mountain stream fed by living springs, the latter a ditch filled from a pump worked by another's hand.

[3] Comenius, John Amos (1592-1670), Czech educational reformer (his Czech name was Jan Komensky) and religious leader, born in Moravia. He was educated at the University of Heidelberg.
[4] Luke 8:11

KNOWLEDGE NECESSARY TO THOUGHT

14. The voluntary action of every mind is limited practically to the field of its acquired knowledge. He who knows nothing cannot think: he has nothing to think about. In comparing, imagining, judging, and reasoning, and in applying knowledge to plan, criticize, express, or execute one's thoughts, the mind must necessarily work upon the material it possesses. Hence the power of any object or truth as a mental excitant depends in each case upon the number of related objects or truths which the mind already knows. A botanist will be aroused to the keenest interest by the discovery of a new plant, but will care little for a new stone or star. The physician studies eagerly new diseases, the lawyer new decisions, the farmer new crops or cattle, the mechanic new structures and machines.

15. The infant knows little, and his interest in any new object is short and slight; the man knows many things, and his interest is deeper, wider, and more persistent. Thoughtfulness deepens and grows intense with increase of knowledge. He who studies mathematics long and deeply never finds this study dry or tiresome, and the wisest student of the Bible finds in its pages the highest delight and gathers there the grandest revelations of supernal truths. All these varying illustrations familiarly show the principles which underlie our law and prove its truth.

TWO EXCITANTS OF THOUGHT

16. The two chief springs of interest through which the mind can be aroused to a voluntary exertion of its powers are the love of knowledge as a mental satisfaction, and the desire of knowledge as a means of obtaining other satisfactions. In the former, or the love of knowledge for its own sake as it is sometimes called, are mingled the satisfaction of the native curiosity of the mind which craves to know the real nature and causes of the phenomena around us, the solution of the unquiet questionings which often trouble the spirit, the relief from apprehensions which ignorance feels in the presence of nature's mysteries, the sense of power and liberty which knowledge often brings, the feeling of mental elevation and superiority which each fresh increment of intelligence gives, and the "rejoicing in the truth"[5] because of its own beauty and sublimity, or its moral charm and sweetness, its appeals to our taste for wit and humor, for the wonderful and the beneficent. All these enter separately or together into the intellectual appetite to which the various forms of knowledge appeal, and which gives to reading and study their highest if not strongest attraction. Each affords an avenue through which the mind can be reached and roused by the skillful teacher.

17. It is evident that this manifold mental appetite must vary in character and intensity with the tastes and attainments of pupils. Some love nature and her sciences of observation

[5] 1 Corinthians 13:6

and experiment; others love the mathematics and delight in their problems; others love languages and literature, and others still history and the spiritual sciences which deal with the powers, doings, and destinies of mankind. Each special appetite grows by feeding, and becomes absorbing as its acquisitions become great. The great masteries and achievements in arts, learning, literature, and science have come from these inborn tastes, and in all these

The child is father of the man.[6]

In each little pupil sleep the germs of such tastes—the coiled springs of such powers—awaiting the art of the teacher to water the germs and set in motion the springs. The natural excitant of each appetite is the offered food of each.

18. The love of knowledge for its uses includes the desire for education as a means of livelihood or as a source of respectability; the felt or anticipated need of some special knowledge, as artist, artisan, lawyer, writer, or other brainworker, as well as the study made to win reward or to avoid punishment and disgrace. This indirect desire for learning varies with the character and aims of the pupil, but does not increase with attainment unless it ripens, as it may, into the true love of knowledge above described. Its strength depends on the nature and largeness of the need which impels to study. The self-activities aroused for such study go to

---

[6] William Wordsworth (1770–1850), *My Heart Leaps Up When I Behold* (1807; written 1802).

a self-imposed task and are little likely to continue their work after the task is done. The rewards and punishments used in school to promote lesson-getting have just this force and no more. They inspire no generous activity which works for the love of the work and which pauses not when its appointed lesson is learned. If the study they induce shall become transfigured into a true love of knowledge, then the violence they do to the pupil's mind may be forgotten; but in most cases they sow disgust in place of generous desire and make all high education harder, if not impossible. Witness the spirit that pervades every school so taught and managed.

THE MORAL INTELLECT

19. Our whole discussion thus far has taken for granted the intimate and indissoluble connection of the intellect and the sensibilities—the inseparable union of thought and feeling. To think without feeling would be thinking with a total indifference to the object of thought, which would be absurd; and to feel without thinking would be to feel without knowing that we feel, which is impossible. Now, as most of the objects of thought are objects also of desire or dislike, and therefore objects of choice, it follows that all important action of the intellect has a moral side or quality; and this, too, has been assumed throughout this volume. This moral side of the intelligence may be called the Moral Intellect, the intellect working in the field of the moral life. The love of knowledge for itself or its uses is moral at bottom, as

it implies moral affections and purposes of good or evil. All motives of study have a moral character or connection, at their first or second step; and hence no education or teaching can be absolutely divorced from morals. The affections and conscience always come to school with the intellect.

20. But the Moral Intellect, or cognitive conscience as we may call it, finds its fuller sphere in the recognized domain of duty—the higher realm of the affections, the virtues, and religion. From these the mind borrows its highest and strongest incentives to study and its clearest light in understanding. Let the teacher constantly address the moral nature and stimulate the moral sentiments, if he wishes to achieve the highest success possible for him.

21. This moral teaching was the chief excellency of Pestalozzi's work, and it is the leading characteristic of every great teacher of mankind. He who would get from the mind of his pupil its highest and most heroic efforts must appeal to its noblest sentiments—its love of God, of its country, and its fellows—its personal aspirations for a noble, useful, and beneficent life—its love for truth and goodness and its purest hopes of heaven. If these sentiments are feeble or wanting, the teacher must build them up, or he will fail in his work.

THE POWER OF THE SUNDAY SCHOOL

22. The Sunday school ought to be the best and most successful of all schools, because it is openly, freely, and

fearlessly religious. The whole moral and religious nature of the child is open to its work. Its education ought therefore to dominate, inspire, and consecrate all other education.

23. Through the Sunday school, Christianity is free to pour its faith into all other schools. Standing as it does on the moral and social hilltop of the week, it should be able to throw its light along all the path of the children's daily work and studies.

24. So soon as the Sunday school becomes strong enough and skillful enough in its teachings, it will color and control all learning with its own higher ideas and hopes. The true interests of mankind, as well as the progress and final success of Christianity itself, demand that this shall be done. Science will cease to be infidel or skeptic when its students shall be good Bible scholars. Witness Newton, Hugh Miller, Agassiz, and Dana, second to none as scientists, but never skeptic, because trained in religious knowledge.

THE MIND DOES ITS OWN WORK

25. It follows from all this that only when the mental powers work free and in their own way can the product be sure or permanent. No one can know what any mind contains, or what labor it performs, save as that mind imperfectly reveals it by words or acts, or as we conjecture it by reflecting on our own conscious experience. Into the sealed workshop of the soul no spectator enters. What the occupant does there no one but himself can tell. Working by his own light on

materials furnished by his own senses and gathered by his own intelligence, it is his to mould, shape, combine, and construct as he will. Just as the digestive organs must do their own work, masticating and digesting whatever food they can get, selecting, secreting, assimilating, and so building bone, muscle, brain, nerve, skin, and all the various tissues and organs of the body; so, too, in the last resort, the mental faculties must do theirs, without external aid, building as they can, opinions, beliefs, purposes, faiths, and all the forms of intelligence and character. As Milton expressed it:

> The mind is its own place, and in itself
> Can make a heaven of hell, a hell of heaven.[7]

26. If I thus emphasize the fact of each mind's autocracy, it is not to belittle the teacher's work, but to show more clearly the law which gives that work all its force and dignity. It is the teacher's mission to stand at the impassable gateways of young souls, a wiser and stronger soul than they, serving as a herald of science, a guide through nature, to summon the faculties within to their work, to place before them the facts to be observed, and to guide them to the paths to be trodden. It is his by sympathy, by example, and by every means of influence—by objects for the senses, by facts for the intelligence, by pictures for the imagination, by stories for the fancy

[7] Milton, John (1608-1674), great English poet around Shakespeare's time. No doubt a favorite author of Gregory's parents, seeing that they gave him the name.

and the heart, to excite the mind, stir the curiosity, stimulate the thoughts, and send them forth as warriors, armed and eager for the conflict. Every thoughtful and observant teacher has had occasion to note the various and original ways in which different pupils will reach the answer to a question, or other mental result, when left to themselves.

27. The cautionary clause of our law which forbids giving too much help to pupils will be needless to the teacher who clearly sees his proper work, and who is eager only to get his pupil's mind into free and vigorous action. Like a skillful engineer who knows the power of his engine, he chooses to stand and watch the play of the splendid machine and marvel at the ease and vigor of its movements. It is only the unskillful and self-seeking teacher who prefers to hear his own voice in endless talk, rather than watch the working of his pupil's thoughts.

28. There is no real disagreement between this law and the first and third, which so strongly insist on the teacher's knowledge of his subject and on his use of familiar language. Only through his own full knowledge of the subject can he understand the difficulties met by the pupil, or be able to determine when the pupil has mastered the lesson, and to follow it with thorough drills and reviews. As well insist that a general need know nothing of a battlefield because he is not to do the actual fighting, as that a teacher may get on with slight knowledge because his pupils must do the studying.

Besides, there are some exceptions to the rule to tell the pupil nothing which he can discover for himself. There come occasions when the teacher may, for a few minutes, turn lecturer or preacher, and before a class well prepared to receive it may, from the stores of his own riper studies, give them broader, richer, and clearer views of the field of their work. He may, for a little, lift the child to his own strong shoulders to give it a clearer view of the path it has traveled, or an inspiring and guiding glimpse of the roadway yet to come; only he must take care not to substitute telling for true teaching, and thus encourage lazy listening where he needs to call for earnest work.

QUESTIONS AS EXCITANTS

29. The chief excitants which nature uses to stir the minds of men have already been noticed. They might all be described as the silent but ceaseless questions which the universe addresses to the spirit of man. The strange and endless questionings which an active child presses upon its often wearied parents are but the echoes of those which nature presses upon its young intellect. The true stimulant of the human mind is a question, and the object or event that does not raise any question will stir no thought. Questioning is not, therefore, merely one of the modes of teaching, it is the whole of teaching; it is the excitation of the self-activities to their work of discovering truth, learning facts, knowing the

unknown. Nature always teaches thus. But it is not necessary that every question shall be in the interrogative form. The strongest and clearest affirmation may have all the effect of the sharpest interrogation, if the mind be sufficiently aroused to so receive it. An explanation may be so given as to raise new questions while it answers old ones.

30. The explanation that settles everything, and ends all questions, ends also all thinking; on that subject at least for the time and in that direction. After a truth is clearly understood, or a fact is established, there still remain its consequences, applications, and uses to be inquired into. And each fact and truth thoroughly studied leads us into the presence of other facts and truths, which renew the questionings and demand fresh investigations. The thoroughly alert and scientific mind is one that never ceases to ask questions and seek answers. The scientific spirit is the spirit of tireless inquiry and investigation. The nineteenth century, which so far excels all its predecessors in the extent of its sciences and arts, excels them also in the number and reach of its questionings. It is above all others the century of great questions.

31. And as with the world, so with the child: his intellectual education fairly begins so soon as he commences earnestly to ask questions. It is only when the questioning spirit has been fully awakened, and the power and habit of raising questions have been largely developed, that the teaching process may give way to the lecture plan, and the

student may be turned into the listener. The truth asks its own questions so soon as the mind is sufficiently awake. The falling apple had the question of universal gravitation in it for the mind of Newton; and the boiling teakettle propounded to James Watt[8] the problem of a steam engine.

Rules for Teachers

Like our other laws, this one also suggests some practical rules for teaching.

1.   Adapt lessons to the ages and tastes of the children. Young pupils will be interested in whatever appeals to the senses; only the mature minds will enter heartily into the truths of reason and reflection.

2.   Select lessons which relate to the present circumstances and wants of pupils. The mind is already awake for these. The story of Lazarus will easily engage the attention of one who has just lost a friend, or been to a funeral.

3.   Consider carefully the subject and the lesson to be taught, and find its points of interest for your own pupils.

4.   Excite the pupil's interest in the lesson when it is given out, by some question or by some statement which will awaken inquiry. Hint that something worth knowing is to be found out if the lesson is thoroughly studied, and be sure to ask for the truth discovered.

[8] Watt, James (1736-1819), Scottish engineer, considered one of the most influential figures of the Industrial Revolution because of his improvements to the steam engine.

5.   Place yourself frequently in the position of a pupil among pupils, and join in the search for some fact or truth, or for the meaning of a text.

6.   Repress the impatience which cannot wait for the pupil to explain himself, and which takes the words out of his mouth. He will resent it, and tell his comrades, if not you, that he could have answered if you had given him time.

7.   In all class exercises aim to excite constantly fresh interest and activity. Start questions for the pupils to investigate out of the class. The lesson that does not end in fresh questionings ends wrong.

8.   Observe each pupil to see that his mind is neither so wandering nor weary as to forbid its activities being bent to the lesson in hand.

9.   Count it your chief duty to "wake up mind," and rest not till each pupil shows his mental activity by asking questions in turn.

10. Repress the desire to tell all you know or think upon the lesson or subject; and if you tell something to illustrate or explain, let it start a fresh question.

11. Give the pupil time to think, after you are sure his mind is actively at work, and encourage him to ask questions when puzzled.

12. Do not answer too promptly the questions asked, but restate them, to give them greater force and breadth, and often answer with new questions to secure deeper thought.

13. Teach pupils to ask *What? Why?* and *How?*—the nature, cause, and method of every fact observed or told them; also *Where? When? By whom?* and *What of it?*—the place, time, actors, and consequences of events.

14. Recitations should not exhaust a subject, but leave work on hand for the class to think out.

VIOLATIONS AND MISTAKES

Many a teacher neglecting these plain rules kills all interest in his class, and wonders how he did it.

(1) The chief and almost constant violation of this law of teaching is the attempt to force lessons into pupils' minds by simply telling. "I have told you ten times, and yet you don't know!" exclaimed a teacher of this sort. Poor teacher, can you not remember that knowing comes by thinking, not by telling? Better the school tyrant who whips his pupils into learning their own lessons than a teacher who tells them all.

(2) It is another mistake to complain of memory for not keeping what it never fairly held. The only cure for a bad memory is to mix more thinking in one's learning. The fact that is seen or read without thought will be forgotten in an hour; but think deeply about a fact for ten minutes, and the chances are that it will be fresh in memory ten years later.

(3) A third violation of the law comes from the hurry

which leads teachers to require prompt and rapid recitations in the very words of the book; and, if a question is asked in the class, to refuse the pupils time to think. If the pupil hesitates and stops for lack of thought, or from fault of memory, which is also lack of thought, the evil lies in yesterday's teaching which shows its fruit today; but if it comes from the slowness of the pupil's thinking, or from the real difficulty of the subject, then time should be given for thought; and, if the lesson hour will not allow it, let the answer go over to the morrow.

It is to this hurried and unthinking lesson-saying that we owe the superficial and impractical character of so much of our school learning. For the noble advice of Paul, to "read, mark, learn, and inwardly digest"[9] the truth, we have substituted the rule, "Learn so as to recite promptly." Thus the word remains "unmixed with faith in those who have it,"[10] and it is as the seed sown by the wayside, which the birds snatch away.[11] If these are bad faults in our day schools, how much more serious in the Bible schools, where the truths studied are

[9] The phrase is actually found, not in Paul, but in the Collect for the Second Sunday in Advent from the Book of Common Prayer (1662): "Blessed Lord, who hast caused all holy Scriptures to be written for our learning; Grant that we may in such wise hear them, read, mark, learn, and inwardly digest them, that by patience and comfort of thy holy Word, we may embrace, and ever hold fast, the blessed hope of everlasting life, which thou hast given us in our Saviour Jesus Christ. Amen."

[10] Hebrews 4:2

[11] Luke 8:5

wider and grander in themselves, and where the lessons have their great use in their applications to the mind, heart, and conscience of the learner. If it is true that there resides in God's Word power to convert the soul, to purify the life, to make wise the simple, and to judge the world, how inexcusable the folly of the teaching which leaves its truths unknown, and sheathes its sharp and glittering blade in the scabbard of a text familiar to the ear but shut to the understanding and the heart!

How different is the result where this great law of teaching is understood and obeyed! The stimulated activities make the scene radiant as with flashing light. The schoolroom is transformed under their power into a busy laboratory of thought and emotion. The pupils become thinkers—discoverers. They master great truths, and apply them to the questions of life and duty. They invade new fields of knowledge. The teacher does but lead the march. Their reconnaissance becomes a conquest. Skill and power grow with their exercise. Mind awakens to its high birthright, and the scholar of the schooltime becomes the student of a lifetime.

VII

THE LAW OF THE
LEARNING PROCESS

1. We must now pass again from the side of the teacher to the side of the learner. It has been seen that the teacher's work consists essentially in arousing and guiding the self-activities of the pupil. The pupil's work, which now demands study, is the use of those self-activities in getting his lesson. The laws of teaching and learning may seem at first to be only different aspects of the same law, but they are quite distinct—the one applying to the work of the instructor, the other to that of the instructed. The law of the *teaching process* involves the means by which the self-activities are to be awakened; the law of the *learning process* determines the manner in which these activities shall be employed.

2. If we watch again a child at his studies, and mark carefully what he is to do, we shall easily see that it is not

merely an effort of the attention, nor a vague and aimless exertion of his mental powers, that is required of him. There is a clear and distinct act or process which we wish him to accomplish. It is to form in his own mind, by the use of his own powers, a complete and truthful conception or notion of the facts and truths in the lesson, in all their parts, relations, proofs, and applications. This is the result to which all efforts of teacher and learner must be bent. The Law of the Learning Process may therefore be stated thus:

The learner must reproduce in his own mind the truth to be acquired.

3.   The laws before discussed have addressed themselves chiefly to the teacher: this comes home also to the learner. It brings into sight the principles which must guide the student in his studies, and which it is the business of the instructor to emphasize and enforce. While telling the teacher how to teach, it also tells the learner how to learn. This will appear more clearly in the discussion which follows.

THE PHILOSOPHY OF THE LAW

4.   As that is not true teaching which simply pours out before the pupil the treasures of the teacher's knowledge, so that is not true learning which merely memorizes and repeats the teacher's words and ideas. Vastly more than is commonly understood or believed, the work of education, of acquiring knowledge, is the work of the pupil and not that of the teacher.

This truth has already been affirmed in other connections. It is reaffirmed here as the fundamental notion in the present discussion. Learning is the formation by the learner in his own mind of the conceptions contained in the lesson learned.

5.   We must distinguish between the original discovery of a truth and the learning it from others. Discovery is made by processes of investigation which are commonly slow, tentative, and laborious. Learning comes by processes of interpretation, which are often easy and rapid. Still there is much in common. The learner rediscovers in part the truth he learns. No discovered truth is wholly new. No true learning is wholly a repetition of other men's thoughts. The discoverer borrows largely of truths known to others; the student must add much to the lesson he studies. His constant aim should be to rise from being a learner at other men's feet, to become an independent searcher of truth for himself. Both discoverer and learner must alike be truth-seekers. Both must aim to gain clear and distinct conceptions of it. Both must needs employ in their work the truths already familiar to them, and both must put their learning to use, to find its full power and value. It is indispensable that the learner shall become an investigator.

6.   Learning has several stages of progress which need to be carefully noticed in order that the full meaning of the law shall be seen and understood. They are the following:

First. A pupil may be said to have learned his lesson when he has committed it to memory, and can recite it word for word. This is all that is attempted by many pupils, or required by those teachers who count their work well done if they can secure such verbatim recitations. Education would be cheap if such learning could be made to stay; but it passes away like the images from a mirror, unless fixed by almost endless repetitions.

Second. It is an evident advance over the memorizing of words when the pupil adds a clear understanding of the thought. So much better is this learning than the other that thoughtful teachers are tempted to say to their pupils: "I do not care for the words of the lesson; give me the thought." But in many cases, especially in Bible lessons, it is important to know and remember the very words.[1]

Third. It is a higher stage in study when the thought is so mastered and measured, as it were, that the pupil can translate it accurately into other words with no loss of meaning. He who can do this has advanced beyond the mere work of learning, and has begun the work of discovering. He is dealing not merely with another's thought of the truth, but with the truth itself. The wise teacher will recognize this, and will pardon the crudeness in expression, while he encourages the pupil to more accurate thinking as a means to more correct language.

Fourth. The learner shows higher work still when he begins

---

[1] "Every word of God is pure: He is a shield unto them that put their trust in Him." (Proverbs 30:5.)

to seek the evidences of the statements which he studies. He who can give a reason for the faith which is in him is a much better learner, as well as stronger believer, than the man who believes, he knows not why. The true investigator seeks proofs, and a large part of the work of a student of nature is to prove the truths which he discovers. So also ought the Bible student to "search the Scriptures"[2] to see for himself if these things are so. Even the youngest learner takes a stronger hold of the truth if he can see a reason for it. In hunting for proofs, the student comes in sight of a hundred other truths, just as one who climbs a mountain finds the landscape always widening around him. The little lesson he is learning is seen to be a part of the great empire of the all-truth; its truth grows clearer in the reflected light of other truths, and the heart, like that of the mountain traveler, revels in the splendid outlook and in the consciousness of growing power.

Fifth. But there is a still higher and more fruitful stage in learning. It is found in the study of the uses and applications of knowledge. No lesson is learned to its full and rich ending till it is traced to its connections with the great working machinery of nature and of life. Nature is not an idle show, nor is the Bible a mass of old wives' fables. Every fact has its uses, and every truth its applications, and till these are found the lesson lies idle and useless as a wheel out of gear with its fellows in the busy machinery. The practical relations of truth,

[2] Acts 17:11

and the forces which lie hid behind all facts, are never really understood till we apply our knowledge to some of the practical purposes of life and thought. The boy who finds a use for his lesson becomes doubly interested and successful in his studies. What was idle knowledge, only half understood, becomes practical wisdom full of zest and power. Especially is this true of Bible knowledge, whose superficial study is of slight effect, but whose profounder learning changes the whole man. "The letter killeth; the spirit giveth life."[3]

7.   No learning is complete till these five stages are passed. They are like five windows of increasing size, each of which pours its fuller light in succession upon the lesson. The first shows it in dim outline only, like an object seen at twilight without distinctness of form or color. The others give increasing clearness to the view, till the gathered illumination of them all makes the truth to stand forth in all its grandeur and beauty, a landscape complete and rich, in colors, forms, and life. Such is the reproduction of the lesson which our law demands, and to this must the efforts of teacher and pupil be steadily bent.

8.   The earnest student will find in these five stages of study the clearest directions for the work he has to do. Let him ask himself: (1) What does the lesson say, word for word? (2) Exactly what does it mean? (3) How express this meaning in my own language? (4) Is the lesson true; in what sense and

[3] 2 Corinthians 3:6

why? (5) What is the good of it—how apply and use the knowledge it gives? It is along these five steps that the learner must mount, if at all, to a broad and clear conception of the full significance and value of the truth learned.

9.   It is true that not many lessons are learned with this comprehensive thoroughness, and it may be that only the briefest and simplest lessons can be so mastered at a single sitting; but this does not change the fact that no lesson can be counted as fully learned till so mastered and understood. Better one subject so learned than a whole curriculum skimmed with lighter study. "Better to know one thing than not to know a hundred." "It is worth more," said the wise Seneca, "to be possessed of but few of the lessons of wisdom, but to apply these diligently, than to know many but not to have them at hand."[4] Such knowledge, and such alone, is power. Truth so studied cleaves to the memory, quickens the intellect, fires the heart, shapes the character, and transforms the life.

THE TWO LIMITATIONS

10. Two limitations to this law of learning need to be considered. *First.* That of the age and powers of the learner. Each of the five stages may be climbed by the youngest as well as by the oldest pupil, but on a path answering to the pupil's

[4] Seneca (possibly 4 BC-65 AD), renowned Roman philosopher, rhetorician, dramatist and statesman born in Cordoba, Spain. He wrote a great deal of ethically based philosophy, of the Stoic variety, during what is known as the Silver Age of Latin literature.

active powers. (1) The mental activity of young children lies close to the senses. Their thinking is a sort of mental seeing. It pictures rather than thinks. Their knowledge of a lesson will be confined chiefly to the facts in it which appeal to the eye, or which can be illustrated to the senses. Many subjects are, of course, beyond their comprehension, but in the subjects which can be taught to them at all, the expression, the meaning, the proofs, and the uses can be shown to their understanding. (2) From ten to fourteen years of age, the imagination is the most active power, and the lesson will be best and most easily learned which can be pictured to the fancy or turned into a plan for some active effort or enterprise. (3) Later the reason begins to assume sway, and the lesson will appeal most to the mind if it asks reasons and gives conclusions. Each great subject of human knowledge will be found to have these three stages of truth in it, and to offer, therefore, some lessons for all ages of learners.

Second. The other limitation is that which comes from the kinds of knowledge. Science, history, art, and Scripture, each has its own evidences and its own uses and applications. In each case the law of learning or study varies to meet conditions. Let the intelligent teacher take a simple example of each sort, and he will easily note the differences and find the true conditions of successful study of each. The student whose powers or methods of study best meet the conditions of learning in any branch of knowledge, easily excels in that branch. Examples are common.

11. Hermann Krüsi, one of the most sagacious of teachers because one of the most sympathetic students of childhood, said:

> Every child that I have ever observed, during all my life, has passed through certain remarkable questioning periods which seem to originate from his inner being. After each had passed through the early time of lisping and stammering, into that of speaking, and had come to the questioning period, he repeated at every new phenomenon the question, "What is that?" If for answer he received the name of a thing, it completely satisfied him; he wished to know no more. After a number of months, a second state made its appearance, in which the child followed its first question with a second: "What is there in it?" After some months more, there came of itself the third question: "Who made it?" and lastly, the fourth: "What do they do with it?" These questions had much interest for me, and I spent much reflection upon them. In the end it became clear to me that the child had struck out the right method for developing its thinking faculties. In the first question, "What is that?" he was trying to get a consciousness of the thing lying before him. By the second, "What is there in it?" he was trying to perceive and understand its interior, and its general and special, marks. The third, "Who made it?" pointed toward the origin and creation of the thing; and the fourth, "What do they do with it?" evidently points at the use and design of the thing. Thus this series of questions seemed to me to include in itself the complete system of mental training. That this originated with the child is not only no objection to it, but is a strong indication that the laws of

thought are within the nature of the child, in their simplest and most ennobling form.

Krüsi's questions belong chiefly to the first period of growth and education. In the second and third periods other questions follow.

PRACTICAL RULES FOR TEACHERS AND LEARNERS

The rules which follow from this law are useful for both teacher and pupil.

1.   Help the pupil to form a clear idea of the work to be done, in its several parts and stages.

2.   Warn him that the words of his lesson have been carefully chosen; that they may have peculiar meanings, which it may be important to find out.

3.   Show him that there are always more things implied than are said in any lesson.

4.   Ask him to express, in simple words of his own, the meaning as he understands it, and to persist till he has the whole thought.

5.   Let the reason why be perpetually asked till the pupil is brought to feel that he is expected to give a reason for his opinions; but let him also understand clearly that reasons must vary with the nature of the truth taught.

6.   Aim to make the pupil an independent investigator—a student of nature, a seeker for truth. Cultivate in him a fixed

and constant habit of research.

7.   Help him to test his conceptions to see that they exactly reproduce the truth taught, in its widest aspects and relations, as far as his powers permit.

8.   Inculcate constantly a profound regard for truth as something noble, enduring and divine—something that God loves and all true and good men revere.

9.   Let it be seen and felt that truth in facts, truth in feeling, truth in words, and truth in action all come under the same eternal and divine law, and that the honest truth-seeker will seek them all alike earnestly.

10.   Teach the pupil to hate all falsehoods, sophistries, and shams as things that are odious, hurtful, dishonoring, shameful, cowardly, and intensely mean and wicked. Make him to dread a false answer to a problem as a lie from the lips.

VIOLATIONS AND MISTAKES

The violations of this law of the learning process are perhaps among the most common and most fatal of any in our school work. Just because this work of learning is the very center of the school work—that for which all else is undertaken—therefore a failure here is a failure in all. Knowledge may be placed before the minds of the young in endless profusion and in the most attractive guise; teachers may pour out instruction without stint, and lessons may be learned and recited under all the pressure of the most effective discipline and of the strongest appeals; but if this law is disobeyed, the teaching is fruitless and the attainments will be short-lived and delusive. Some of the more common mistakes are these:

(1) The pupil is left in the twilight of an imperfect and fragmentary knowledge by a failure to think it into clearness. The haste to get forward often precludes time for thinking.

(2) The language of the book is so insisted on that the pupil is forbidden to try his own power of expression. Thus the student is taught to feel that the word is everything, the meaning nothing. College students have been known to learn the demonstrations of geometry by heart, and never to suspect any meaning in them.

(3) The failure to insist upon original thinking by the pupils is one of the most common faults of our schools. A really thoughtful scholar is the rare exception in most schools.

(4) Commonly no reason is asked for the statements in the lesson, and none is given. The pupil is taught to believe what the book says, and because the book says it. Thus the reason is dwarfed by disuse, and gives no help in study except in following the book. Not knowing how to prove his thought true when it is true, he is unable to detect its falsehood when false.

(5) The applications of knowledge are persistently

neglected. That his lesson has a use, and that he can apply it to some practical purpose, is the last thought to enter the minds of many pupils. The examples of this fault are too many and too common to need further detail here.

Nowhere are these faults in teaching more frequent or more serious in their consequences than in the Sunday school. "Always learning, but never able to come to a knowledge of the truth,"[5] tells the sad story of many a Sunday school class. Let that class be taught for six months as our law prescribes; let the pupils penetrate beyond the letter to the deep meaning of the texts; let the splendid truths of religion in all their breadth of meaning be pondered, proved, and applied, and its whole character would be changed. Faith would follow hearing; frivolity would give place to the deepest earnestness, and the truth of God would vindicate its divine origin by the exhibition of its transforming power.

[5] 2 Timothy 3:7

VIII

THE LAW OF REVIEW

1. Let us suppose the ordinary process of teaching to be finished. The teacher and pupil have met and have done their work together. Language freighted with ideas and aided with illustrations has been uttered and understood. Knowledge with its treasures of truth has been thought into the mind of the learner, and it lies there in greater or less completeness, to feed thought, to guide conduct, and to form character. What more is needed? The teacher's task seems ended. But no! The most delicate, if not also the most difficult, work remains to be accomplished. All that has been done lies hidden in the learner's mind, and lies there as a potency rather than a possession. What eye shall penetrate the understanding to determine the clearness and accuracy of the pupil's cognitions? What hand shall nurse into larger growth and

into permanent force the ideas he has been led to conceive? What process shall fix into active habits the thought-potencies which have been evolved? It is for this final and finishing work that our seventh and last law provides. This Law of the Test, of the confirmation and ripening of results, may be expressed as follows:

The completion, test, and confirmation of teaching must be made by reviews.

2. This wording of the law seeks to include the three chief aims of reviews: (1) To perfect knowledge. (2) To confirm knowledge. (3) To render knowledge ready and useful. These three aims, though distinct in idea, are so connected in fact as to be secured by the same process. It would be difficult to overstate the value and importance of this law of reviews. No time in teaching is spent more profitably than that spent in reviewing. Other things being equal, he is the ablest and most successful teacher who secures from his pupils the most frequent, thorough, and interesting reviews.

PHILOSOPHY OF THE LAW

3. A review is something more than a repetition. A machine may repeat a process, but only an intelligent agent can review it. The repetition done by a machine is a second movement precisely like the first; a repetition by the mind is the rethinking of a thought. It is necessarily a review. It is more: it involves fresh conceptions and new associations, and

brings an increase of facility and power.

4.   Reviews are of different grades of completeness and thoroughness, from the mere repetition of the words of bygone lessons, or a rapid glance thrown back to some fact or phrase, to the most careful resurvey of the whole field—the occupancy in full force of the ground of which the first study was only a reconnaissance. The first and simplest reviews are mostly repetitions; the final and complete reviews should be thorough re-studies of the lessons.

5.   A partial review may embrace a single lesson, or it may include a single branch of the subject—the development of a single truth, the recall of some one fact or event, or of some difficult point or question. The complete review may be a cursory reviewing of the whole field in a few general questions, or it may be a full and final reconsideration of the whole ground. Each form of review has its place and use. The value and real character of a true review will appear in the discussion. We shall see that no teaching can be complete without the review, made either under the teacher's direction, or voluntarily by the scholar himself.

6.   A new lesson or fresh subject never reveals all its truth on a first study of it. Its novelties dazzle the mind and distract the attention. When we enter a strange house, we know not where to look for its several rooms, and the attention is drawn to a few of the more singular and conspicuous features of furniture. We must return again and again, and resurvey the

scene with eyes grown familiar to the place and to the light, before the whole plan of the building and the uses of all the rooms with their furniture will stand clearly revealed. So one must return again and again to a lesson if he would see all there is in it, and come to a true and vivid understanding of its meaning. We have all noticed how much we find that is new and interesting in reading again some old and familiar volume.

7.   Even in the best studied book, we are often surprised to find fresh truths and new meanings in passages which we had pondered again and again without seeing. It is the ripest student of Shakespeare who finds most of freshness in the works of the great dramatist. The familiar eye discovers in any great masterpiece of art or literature touches of power and beauty which the casual observer cannot see. So a true review always adds something to the knowledge of the student making it. The practiced mind finds truths which the first study did not reveal.

8.   Especially is this true of the Bible, of which the last study is always the richest and most interesting. Nothing more surprises or delights us in the great preachers than the new meanings they discover in old and familiar texts—meanings which we are obliged to confess lie clearly there, but which our careless reading had prevented us from finding. Sometimes these meanings lie hidden in a word, and need only the right emphasis to reveal them; sometimes they lie close by the path and appear by some sidelight skillfully

thrown upon them from the text. If any one wishes to try this for himself, let him take some familiar passage, the first verse of the Bible for example, and recite it, first in the rapid and careless way a child would usually say it, then repeat it several times slowly and solemnly, with varying emphasis, and with all the thought and feeling he can summon; somewhat as here indicated:

In the beginning God created the heaven and the earth.

Now read with longer pauses and deeper thinking:

In—the beginning—God—created—the heaven—and—the earth.

Then more slowly, pausing and concentering the whole power of thought on the words marked for emphasis:

In the BEGINNING—God created the heaven and the earth.

In the beginning—GOD—created the heaven and the earth.

In the beginning—God—CREATED—the heaven and the earth.

In the beginning God created—the HEAVEN—and the earth.

IN—THE BEGINNING—GOD—CREATED—

THE HEAVEN—AND—THE EARTH.

What a world of meaning at last rolls along with the resounding words! How wondrously in that remote and awful beginning, where the Deity stands alone with His eternal wisdom, power, and glory, the peopled heavens and the green earth move forth from the creating hand of God, and begin the long march of geologic and historic time!

9.   On one occasion at least, the Great Teacher Himself

resorted to this power of repetition, when three times in succession He asked Peter the question: "Lovest thou Me?"[1] The heart of the rock disciple burned as with fire under this powerful iteration, and with memory and conscience quickened he appealed to the omniscience of his Master to witness to the truth of his questioned love.

10. But the repetitions of a review are not made the same hour. They are spread over days and weeks, and hence they bring a new element into play. The lapse of time changes the point of view. At every review we survey the lesson from a new standpoint. Its facts rise in a new order and are seen in new relations. Truths that stood in the shadow in the first study come forth into the light. When one climbs a mountain, from each successive opening and outlook the eye visits again the same landscape, but the observer's position is always changed. The features of the landscape are seen in different perspective, and each successive view is larger, more comprehensive, and more complete than its predecessor.

11. The human mind does not achieve its victories by a single effort. There is a sort of mental incubation by which frequently, from some common fact, the eagle form of a splendid discovery springs forth. The physiologists call it unconscious cerebration, by which they mean that the brain itself goes on working all unknown to us, and works out new truths from the facts we have learned. It is an easier if not also

[1] John 21:15-17

a truer explanation that the ever advancing and growing mind reaches constantly new positions, and obtains new light by which the new truth becomes visible. Some fresh experience or newly acquired idea serves as a key to the old lesson, and what was dark in the first study is made clear and bright in the review. The mind, like an artist, sketches its pictures at first simply in outline, and in detached parts. Only after many returns to each part do its conceptions stand forth in full light and shade, perfect paintings, lifelike and complete.

12. The old saying, "Beware of the man of one book,"[2] has this in it, that his repeated readings of his one book give him a mastery of the subject which makes him a dangerous antagonist on his chosen field. He but shows the power conferred by frequent reviews.

13. The memory, too, requires frequent repetitions as the essential condition of its retentive holding, and its ready recall of its treasures. Memory depends wholly on the association of ideas—the idea in mind recalling the ideas with which it has been linked by some past association. Each review establishes new associations, while it familiarizes and strengthens the old. The lesson that is studied but once is learned only to be forgotten. That which is thoroughly and repeatedly reviewed is woven into the very fabric of our thoughts, and becomes a part of our permanent knowledge. Not what a pupil has once learned and recited, but what he permanently remembers is

[2] St. Thomas Aquinas (1225-1274).

the true measure of his advance. One fact well remembered is of more worth than a hundred forgotten.

14. Not merely to know, but to have knowledge for use—to possess it fully, like coin for daily traffic, or like tools and materials for daily work—such is the true aim of study. This readiness of knowledge can never be gained by a single study. Frequent and thorough reviews can alone give the mind this firm hold and free handling of the truth. There is a skill in scholarship as well as in handicrafts, and this skill in both cases depends upon habits; and habit is the child of repetition.

15. The plastic power of truth in shaping conduct and molding character belongs only to the truths which have become familiar by repetitions. Not the scamper of a passing child but the repeated tread of going and coming feet beats for us the paths of our daily life. If we would have any great truth sustain and control us, we must return to it so often that it will at last rise up in mind as a dictate of conscience, and pour its steady light upon every act and purpose with which it is concerned.

16. The well-known influence of maxims and proverbs comes from the readiness with which they are remembered and recalled, and the power they gather by repetition. So the texts of Scripture which most influence us are those that have become familiar by use, and which arise in mind as occasions demand. Thousands have been converted by the well-remembered text on whom the sermon made no impression.

17. From all this it will be seen that the review is not simply an added excellency in teaching which may be dispensed with if time is lacking, but it is one of the seven essential conditions of all true teaching. Not to review is to leave the work half done, to fade out with the passing hour. The law of review rests upon the universal and unchangeable laws of mind. The review may not always be made formally and with clear design, but no successful teaching was ever done in which the review in some form, either by direction of the teacher or by the private impulse of the learner, did not take place—the revisiting and repetition of the lesson learned. The "line upon line and precept upon precept"[3] rule of the Bible is a recognition of this truth.

18. The processes of review must necessarily vary with the subject of study, and also with the age and advancement of the pupils. With very young pupils the review can be little more than a simple repetition; with older students, the review will be a thoughtful re-study of the ground to gain deeper understanding.

A principle in mathematics may be reviewed with fresh applications and problems. A scientific truth may be fixed by the study or analysis of a fresh specimen, or by additional facts proving the same truth. A chapter in history may be restudied with fresh questions calling for a fresh view, or by comparing it with the fresh statements of another author. A Scripture truth will be reviewed by a new application to the

[3] Isaiah 28:10, 13

heart and conscience or to the judgment of the duties and events of the life.

19. In the Bible more than in any other book are reviews needful and valuable. Not only does the Bible most require and most repay repeated study, but most of all ought Bible knowledge to be familiar to us, if it be, as is claimed, the Word of God. Its great truths ought to dwell in the heart and in the conscience as a divine presence; its very language should haunt the memory as echoes from the hills of heaven. Its words and precepts should rest clear and precise in the thoughts as the dictates of duty and the prophecies of destiny. Its grand and divine doctrines, its august and vital precepts, its blessed promises, its sublime histories, and still sublimer prophecies, ought to inhabit the mind as heavenly and familiar guests, or rather as divine forces bearing with a constant and molding pressure upon all the acts and decisions of our lives. It is that part of the Bible which thus lives within us, not the great volume which lies upon the table or shelf, which is the true Word of God to us—the daily bread of our Godward life.

20. Any exercise may serve for a review which recalls the truth to be reviewed. One of the best and most practical forms of review is the calling up of any fact or truth learned and applying it to some use. Nothing so fixes it in the memory or gives such a grasp of it to the understanding. Thus the multiplication table may be learned by orderly repetitions of its successive factors and products, but its frequent review and

use in daily computations alone give us that perfect mastery of it which makes it come, as it were, without call, and serve us as if a native part of the mind itself. So in that largest, most wonderful because most arbitrary, and yet most perfect, acquisition of the human mind—the thousands of wholly artificial word-signs and idioms of the mother tongue— nothing but the ceaseless repetitions and reviews of daily use could so bed them in the memory and so in-work them into the habitudes of the mind that they come with the ideas they symbolize and keep pace with the swift movements of thought itself, as if a natural part of the thinking process.

21. The ready skill of artisans and professional men in recalling instantaneously the principles and processes of their arts or professions is the product of the innumerable repetitions of daily practice. This kind of review is available in all cases in which the learner can be called upon to apply the truths learned to the answer of common questions, the solution of problems, the conduct of any process, or the performance of any series of acts. The art of the teacher, in this work, lies in the starting of questions or finding which shall require the use of the knowledge he wishes to have reviewed.

22. The use of the pen and pencil in review work ought by no means to be forgotten. Next to the eye, the hand is the born teacher of the mind, and no reviews are more effective than those which the hand helps. Witness the power of the laboratory work, now so common in all scientific study. The

ingenious teacher will easily find handwork for pen or pencil in any branch of learning. The request for the pupils to bring lists of persons, objects, places, dates, or distances mentioned in the lessons gone over, for tabular statements of facts or events, for maps, plans, or drawings of places or things, or for short written statements or answers, will set a review in progress of no mean value.

23. In Bible lessons these pen and pencil reviews are peculiarly easy and valuable. Its biographies, histories, and geography—its doctrines, promises, precepts, and duties—its parables, miracles, and prophecies—its patriarchs, prophets, priests, judges, kings, apostles, sinners, and saints, and all its marvelous classes and diversities of texts, give endless fields of useful work for the writing hands.

PRACTICAL RULES FOR TEACHERS

Among the many practical rules and methods for reviews, the following are some of the most useful:

1.   Count reviews as always in order. Whenever a spare moment occurs while waiting for other exercises, or when the teacher or class is unprepared to do anything else, a review may go on.

2.   Have also set times for reviews. At the opening of each lesson-hour take a brief review of the preceding lesson, to put the two lessons in connection that no break may occur in the work.

3.   At the close of each lesson give a glance backward to

the ground gone over, and note the points to be especially remembered.

4.   After five or six lessons are past, start a review from the beginning, taking the substance of two or three lessons each day. The order of an exercise may be as follows: *First,* a brief review of the first two lessons, to be followed the next day by the second two, and so on; *second,* a more careful review of the last preceding lesson; *third,* the advance lesson of the day. All this must, of course, be adapted to the time given to the class work. If that is short, the reviews must also be brief. The best teachers give about one third of each lesson-hour to reviews. Thus they make haste slowly but surely.

5.   Whenever a reference can be usefully made to former lessons, the opportunity should be seized to bring forward into fresh light and new connections the old knowledge.

6.   All advance lessons may be made to bring into review truths in former lessons, since the advance in some way depends upon the beginnings.

7.   Make the first review as soon as practicable after the lesson is first learned, before the memory has lost its hold. Afterward occasional reviews will suffice.

8.   In order to make reviews easily and rapidly, the teacher should hold in mind large masses of the lessons learned, ready for instant use. He is thus able to begin at any spare minute an impromptu miscellaneous review on any part of the field; and the pupils, seeing that the teacher thinks it

worthwhile to remember what they have studied, will be ambitious to be ready to meet his questions.

9. New questions started on old lessons, new illustrations for old texts, new proofs for old statements, will often send the pupil back with fresh interest to look again into the old lesson, and he will be thus lured into an unsuspected review.

10. The final review, never to be omitted, should be searching, comprehensive, and masterful, grouping all parts of the subject learned as on a map, and giving the pupil the feeling of a familiar mastery of it all.

11. Seek as many applications as possible of the subject studied. Every thoughtful application involves a useful and effective review.

12. Forget not the value of pencil and pen work in reviews. This work can be done out of class, and it shows for itself.

13. An interesting form of review is to allow members of the class to ask questions on previous lessons. If this is a frequent exercise, the pupils will make volunteer studies both to get questions and to be ready with answers.

Violations and Mistakes

The common and almost constant violations of this last great law of teaching will occur to everyone who reads the foregoing rules and statements. But the disastrous results of these violations are known only to those who have taken thoughtful account of the poor and stinted outcome of all our laborious and costly teaching work. When for the time our pupils should have become teachers they "have need that one teach them again."[4] Forever learning, they seem "never able to come to a knowledge of the truth."[5] And although the lack of reviews is not the sole cause of failures, their thorough use would go far to remedy the evils from other sources. We pour water into broken cisterns: good reviews would stop the leaks, though they might not increase at once the quantity poured in.

The first violation of the law is the total neglect of reviews. This is the folly of the utterly poor and idle teacher.

Second comes the wholly inadequate reviews. This is the fault of the hurried and impatient teacher, who is more anxious to get through the book than to get the book through the mind of his pupils.

The third mistake is that of delaying all reviews till the end of the quarter, when, the lessons being wholly forgotten, the review amounts to a poor and hurried re-learning, with little interest and less profit.

The fourth blunder is that of degrading the review into a lifeless repetition of the same questions and answers as those used at first. This has the form of a review without its power.

The law of reviews in its full force and philosophy requires that there shall be a fresh vision—a clear rethinking of the truths of the lesson, which shall stand related to the first study

[4] Hebrews 5:12
[5] 2 Timothy 3:7

as the artist's finishing-touches stand to his first sketches; or shall be as the final trial and polishing of the weapons with which the pupil is sent forth to the battles of life.

CONCLUSION

I have now finished the discussion of the Seven Laws of Teaching. If I have succeeded in my purpose, I have made to rise up and pass before the reader, *first*, the True Teacher richly laden with the lesson he desires to communicate, inspired and inspiring by the clear vision he has caught of the truth; *second*, the True Learner with attention fixed and interest excited, eager to enter and possess the promised land of the unknown lying before him; *third*, the True Medium of communication between these two—a language clear, simple, and perfectly understood by both; *fourth*, the True Lesson—the knowledge, to the pupil the unknown standing next to his known, and half revealed in its light. These four—the actors and machinery of the drama—have also been shown in action, giving, *fifth*, the True Teaching Process, the teacher arousing and directing the self-activities of the pupil, like a chieftain leading his soldiers into battle; *sixth*, the True Learning Process, the pupil reproducing in thought—thinking into his own mind, step by step—first in mere outline and finally in full and finished conception—the lesson to be learned; and *seventh*, the True Reviews, testing, correcting, completing, connecting, and fixing into permanence, power, and use the subject studied. In all this there has been seen only the play of the great natural laws of mind and of truth effecting and governing that complex process by which a human intelligence gains possession of any branch of knowledge. The study of these laws may not make of every reader a perfect teacher; but the laws themselves, when fully observed in use, will produce their effects with the same certainty that the chemic laws generate the compounds of chemical elements, or that the laws of life produce the growth of the body.

Index

Index

Index

Index

Index

Index

Index